David Crookes

Facebook
for Seniors

In easy steps is an imprint of In Easy Steps Limited
16 Hamilton Terrace · Holly Walk · Leamington Spa
Warwickshire · United Kingdom · CV32 4LY
www.ineasysteps.com

Notice of Liability
Every effort has been made to ensure that this book contains accurate
and current information. However, In Easy Steps Limited and the
author shall not be liable for any loss or damage suffered by readers
as a result of any information contained herein.

Trademarks
All trademarks are acknowledged as belonging to their respective
companies including the images used for illustrative purposes.

In Easy Steps Limited supports The Forest Stewardship Council (FSC),
the leading international forest certification organization. All our titles
that are printed on Greenpeace approved FSC certified paper carry the
FSC logo.

MIX
Paper from
responsible sources
FSC® C020837

Printed and bound in the United Kingdom

ISBN 978-1-84078-822-5

Contents

1 Introducing Facebook

Facebook was launched in 2004, and it has since become the world's most popular social network.

Beware

Only people aged 13 and over can sign up to Facebook.

What is Facebook?

You will have heard a lot about Facebook in day-to-day conversation, on television and in the news. It may even be the reason why you have picked up this book. But if you are still unsure what Facebook is and what it does, then you are not as alone as you may think.

Although Facebook has more than 2.7 billion active monthly users, its large and fast growth over the past decade or so means it has become different things to different people. At its heart, though, Facebook is an online social network, and it allows people to connect with family as well as friends old and new.

By signing up, you can share your experiences and thoughts, and hear those of others. You can post funny stories, photos, videos and web links. You can invite people to events and get involved in Groups. You can buy and sell items; play games; and host video chats. Keeping in touch is easier than it has ever been.

In many ways, Facebook is like a large, virtual room packed with people whose company you enjoy, and it is a great reflection of life. The more friends you connect with, the more enjoyable and useful Facebook becomes.

You can use Facebook on:

- **A computer**: Visit **facebook.com**

- **A mobile phone**: Using apps for Android and iOS.

- **A tablet**: Again, using the Facebook apps.

- **Other devices**: An app called Facebook Watch is available on televisions and videogame consoles as well as Facebook's own Portal device, Amazon Fire TV, Apple TV and Android TV.

Facebook's origins

Facebook was invented by Harvard student Mark Zuckerberg and three of his classmates, Andrew McCollum, Chris Hughes and Dustin Moskovitz. It launched on February 4, 2004 as **thefacebook.com** with the intention of connecting students around their university campus, and it instantly proved to be popular.

The early network allowed users to create a customized profile. Visitors to those profiles could read anything someone had posted and they could also leave messages. This struck a chord with users, who enjoyed the social aspect of the site. Within months, it was being used by students at other US universities too, and by October 2005 it had found its way to the UK as it expanded to colleges and high schools worldwide. Soon, employees at a select number of companies were also invited to join. Momentum was building fast.

Facebook eventually opened to the general public on September 26, 2006. In that same month a News Feed was introduced, and Facebook truly came into its own. The News Feed showed users a list of their friends' activity on the site, allowing for an at-a-glance view of what their connections were up to. It is a feature that remains central to Facebook today, and it has proven to be a crucial component to the network's success.

Since then lots of other features have been added, including Messenger, live streaming, and the ability to make video calls.

All of this has allowed Facebook to become one of the world's largest internet companies. As if to show Facebook's increased worth, Microsoft snapped up a 1.6 percent share in 2007; a move that valued the company at $15 billion. In August 2020, it was roughly valued at $720 billion.

Facebook's key features

When you start using Facebook, you soon realize just how vast and feature-packed it is. It goes beyond simply connecting with your family, friends and acquaintances, even though it is packed with all the tools you need to find and connect with others. Facebook also allows you to:

Share photos and videos

Show your family and friends what you've been up to and keep up-to-date with their lives by sharing photos and videos. You can use images and footage you have previously taken, perhaps of that wonderful holiday of a lifetime, or you can take photos or record something fresh and upload it in seconds. If the photo contains a person, you can associate them with the image, in a process known as tagging. You can also create albums and use images to personalize your profile.

Set up and join Groups

Groups are a perfect way of bringing people together. Perhaps you run a society or you have an interest and want to find like-minded individuals.

Maybe you want to host a reunion of old friends. By setting up a Group or joining one that already exists, you can get involved in discussions, kick around some ideas and find out what's new.

Keep on top of events

Quite aside from being reminded of birthdays, Facebook allows you to send and receive invites to specific events. Many hosts use Facebook to spread the word about their events via posts, photos and videos, and it's possible to discover who can and can't attend. Facebook also includes online-only events so you can get involved with a gathering and keep updated about it without even leaving your home. Be informed of and discover cookery or fitness classes, enjoy talks and check out events across the world.

Create a live broadcast

Out and about and want to share your experiences in real time? With Facebook Live, you can stream video footage from wherever you may be to friends, family or the entire world if you wish. Available on both mobiles and via a webcam on your computer, it has become a popular way to engage with lots of people at once and enjoy feedback from those watching.

Take messaging to another level

Sure – you can use the messaging service built into your phone, but Facebook Messenger is not only convenient; it also lets you contact people even if you don't have their phone number. See who is currently available, create group chats, and even engage with people direct via voice and video calls.

Challenge friends to a game

Facebook has a section dedicated to games and you don't have to play alone. Challenge your friends or family to word-based or card games – just two of the many categories on offer.

Buy and sell items

If you have any items that you need to get rid of or if there is something that you would love to buy, you can make good use of Facebook's Marketplace. With no fees and the ability to sell to your local community, the service gives you the tools to make and save money. It won't take up much of your time either, since the listings are both quick to create and read.

Catch the latest news

Lots of top news outlets have Facebook accounts, and they regularly post links to their top stories. Lively debates are often sparked in the comment sections of these posts, helping gauge the public mood. Readers in the US can also enjoy a dedicated News section. Find it by tapping the menu in the Facebook app for Android and iPhone.

Don't forget

Don't be afraid of trying these Facebook services. They are free (although some events may charge if you attend).

Where Facebook is heading

Facebook is continuing to innovate, ensuring that it will not stand still at any point in the near future. We know this because each year the company holds its F8 developer conference, where it outlines the technology that it is working on. Even when it has not been able to hold the conference, announcements are made. Indeed, the F8 in 2020 was replaced by a series of updates throughout the year.

By getting to grips with Facebook today, you'll be in a position to enjoy whatever Facebook brings tomorrow. Here are some features to look forward to:

A virtual future

You may have heard of Virtual Reality (VR). By donning a headset that covers both of your eyes with screens, and by reacting to your head movements, you can be transported into a digital world ready to be explored.

Facebook bought VR specialists Oculus in 2014 for a total of $2 billion, and the release of its Oculus Quest headset allowed for wireless VR. Facebook showed its commitment to VR by releasing Quest 2 in 2020. But what could it mean for you?

Currently, Facebook is promoting VR for videogames but the technology can bring great health benefits. It can potentially combat social isolation by opening users to new experiences such as virtual excursions to interesting locations. It could allow for trips down memory lane or offer new ways to relax.

An app called Alcove, for example, is available for free for Oculus Go and it allows family members to meet in a virtual space if each one is wearing a headset. You can use this app to travel to wonderful places or even dive in the Great Barrier Reef of Australia. Visit **https://www.oculus.com/experiences/go/2855012877858033/** for more details.

Hot tip

Stay informed of the latest comings and goings from Facebook by visiting its newsroom. You'll find information about new features and initiatives. Go to **https://about.fb.com/news/**

Rise of the bots

We are already seeing the use of bots: software applications programmed to automatically perform tasks over the internet. You can chat with them in Messenger and be easily fooled into believing you are conversing with a real person. But because they can be used to help you with your everyday tasks, and since they can second-guess what you may want, Facebook says you will be seeing a lot more of them.

Less fake news and clickbait

Fake news has become the scourge of social media. It happens when people deliberately create and share information they know to be false. It can be a misleading image, or an entire news article from a rogue website, and it will seek to influence opinion and get you to click.

Facebook is helping reduce the amount of fake news shared on its platform. Users can report articles that can be independently checked. Facebook is also using advanced algorithms to look out for exaggerated information in headlines and for signs that details are being deliberately withheld. What you read on Facebook should be much closer to the truth, but still exercise caution.

Privacy and security

Not only does Facebook ask for personal information such as your date of birth and what you like and don't like; the social network also encourages you to share details about your life. As such, many people have raised concerns about privacy and security, and you will sometimes see articles about this in the news.

Back in 2010, Mark Zuckerberg said privacy was no longer "a social norm" and that people have become used to openly sharing information. It is true that the rise of services such as Facebook and Twitter have shifted the boundaries somewhat, yet there has also been a move toward social media that offers greater privacy and security. The likes of WhatsApp and Snapchat use technology such as end-to-end encryption and disappearing messages. Facebook is committed to end-to-end encryption for messaging.

Who is Mark Zuckerberg?

As we mentioned on page 9, Mark Zuckerberg founded Facebook with the help of three classmates when he was a student at Harvard University. But he has arguably grown just as fast as the social network he created. Today he is the chairman and chief executive officer of the company, and he is said to be worth an estimated

$99.6 billion, making him the fourth-richest person in the world.

Zuckerberg's early days

Zuckerberg was born on May 14, 1984 in White Plains, New York, and he began programming computers in middle school. By the time he went to university, he had produced a program that allowed computers to communicate with each other called ZuckNet, as well as games and a media player.

Creating Facemash

In 2003, while at Harvard, he created a version of Am I Hot or Not? called Facemash. It compared many pairs of student faces and asked the user to decide who was the most stunning. Although it got him into some hot water and was pulled, it encouraged him to move on to different projects. He devoted much of his time to creating Facebook instead, eventually moving to Palo Alto, California, which is at the heart of Silicon Valley.

The rise of Facebook and Zuckerberg

Zuckerberg has had many opportunities to sell Facebook but he has always turned them down, once being quoted as saying his aim was "making the world open". His efforts have seen him meeting many presidents and prime ministers as he seeks to get people communicating the world over, and he has become very well known both in and outside tech circles. He voiced himself in an episode of The Simpsons and there has also been a movie based on his founding Facebook years, called The Social Network.

Zuckerberg's generosity

In 2010, Zuckerberg signed The Giving Pledge, promising that he would, over time, give half of his wealth to charity. On top of that, he has handed far in excess of $1 billion to good causes and he is keen to help stamp out disease.

2 Setting up a new Facebook account

This chapter shows you how to open an account on Facebook, add information and a photograph, and find friends to connect with.

Getting a Facebook account

Facebook allows you to create a single, personal account for free. The sign-up process takes very little time, and you can complete it at **facebook.com** using a web browser on your computer.

Once you have created an account, you will be also able to access Facebook through any browser, smartphone and tablet device that you may own.

Don't forget

Facebook can be used on the web or via an app, and the location of settings and features can differ. We look solely at the desktop version for the first four chapters of this book, before introducing the mobile apps.

1 Visit **facebook.com** and select **Create New Account**

2 Enter your name, your mobile number or email address and create a password

3 Use the drop-down buttons to select your date of birth

4 Now, indicate whether you are female or male, or select **Custom** to select your pronoun and enter your own gender preference

Sign Up   ✕
It's quick and easy.

First name | Surname

Mobile number or email address

New password

Hot tip

Although Facebook asks for your birthday, you will be able to control who sees it later.

16

5 Click the green **Sign Up** button

Confirming your Facebook account

1 You will need to confirm your account before you can use it. Watch out for an email or a text message depending on how you signed up. Make a note of the confirmation code and select **Confirm Your Account**

2 Enter the code on the Facebook website when prompted and select **Continue**. You may be asked if you want your computer or device to remember your password. This will make it easier to log in to Facebook in the future but, for security, never allow this on a public computer

Adding a profile photograph

Adding a photograph of yourself to your Facebook profile is important because it lends a personal touch. It also:

- Helps other people recognize you when you connect.

- Represents you when you write posts and comments.

- Encourages others to feel comfortable chatting to you.

It should be the first thing you do after setting up an account. You could add an old photo, or take and use a new one.

Adding an image you've already taken

1 Look toward the right of the Navigation bar located at the top of the screen. You will see a button containing your name. Select this to visit your profile page

2 To use an existing image stored on your computer, simply click the **Camera** icon on the silhouetted profile image

3 Select **+ Upload Photo**

4 Browse the files on your computer and select the image that you wish to use

5 Position your image within the highlighted circle by dragging it using the on-screen cursor

Hot tip

Close-up shots without a lot of background work best for profile images. That's because the photos display at just 170 x 170 pixels on a computer, and 128 x 128 pixels on a smartphone.

17

Don't forget

Profile images will be automatically cropped to fit a circle.

...cont'd

6 Move the slider beneath the image to the right (toward the **+**) to zoom in on the image or left (toward the **-**) to zoom out

7 Write a description of your image if you wish

8 A profile image is not permanent. You can change it at any time or opt to make it temporary. For the latter, click **Make Temporary** and use the drop-down option tool to indicate how long the image should display for before returning the previous image (in this case, back to the silhouetted profile image). Choose from 1 hour to 1 month or select **Custom** to input a date and time

9 Click **Save**

18

Adding a cover photograph
Cover images can help a profile page stand out. Images are displayed 820 pixels wide and 312 pixels tall on desktops.

1 Click **Add Cover Photo** on your profile page

2 Select **Upload Photo** and find a suitable image by searching through the files on your computer

Completing your About page

Facebook's About page allows you to write a basic profile about yourself. You can use it to share details about your life and interests, and even to let others know how they can contact you.

How much information you impart or keep private is entirely up to you. But there are benefits to giving at least some information away. Certainly, if you have a common name, providing details about your past can help others better identify you.

Adding information about yourself

You can provide an overview of your life by adding a workplace, school/university, current city, home town and relationship status.

1 Click the tab marked **About**

Timeline	About	Friends

2 You will see that **Overview** is highlighted

3 "Plus" icons are located next to each heading. Click them if you wish to add information

4 Fill in the forms as you go down the list, ticking or unticking boxes and using any drop-down menus that you may encounter

5 When you complete each section, click **Save**

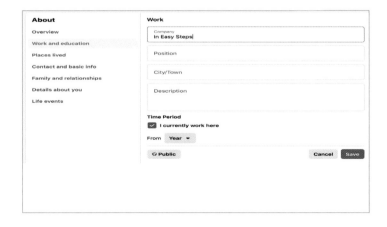

Editing your contact info

As you make your way down the sections of your About page, you should pay special attention to the **Contact and basic info** part. Here, you are able to:

- Input your mobile phone number and home address.

- Add your website and other social media accounts.

- Make alterations to your date of birth.

Adding contact information

1 On the About screen, click **Contact and basic info** on the left-hand menu

2 Click on the links for **Add a mobile phone** and **Add your address**

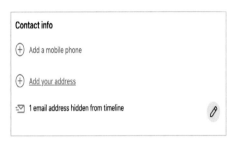

3 Input your details, but click the **Friends** button and choose who should be able to see the information from the list

4 Click **Save**

Adding a website and social link

1 **Add a website** lets you input a web address

2 **Add a social link** lets you link to other social media profiles including Instagram, Twitter and WhatsApp

Hiding personal details

You need to be careful when inputting your personal details. After all, you don't want to give too much away. One of the most important pieces of information you will be asked to give is your date of birth. This will be shown to anyone who clicks About on your profile, but you can determine how it is shown.

Don't change your date of birth too often, otherwise Facebook will force you to wait before you can edit it.

1 On the About screen, click **Contact and basic info** on the left-hand menu

2 Look for the **Basic Info** section

3 Click the **Edit** button next to your birthday

4 Your birthday details will be split over two lines. First you will see the month you were born and the day (as inputted by you). You could decide to mask your real birthday by making up a date but that would mean that people could not wish you a happy birthday

5 Instead, click the box next to the date and decide who should see this information. We would suggest **Friends**

6 You can now move to the year. This is more sensitive so again, click the box next to the year and we would suggest selecting **Only me**. Doing so means no-one will be able to see the year you were born by clicking on your About information. Of course, there would be no harm in making up a year either and keeping that private too

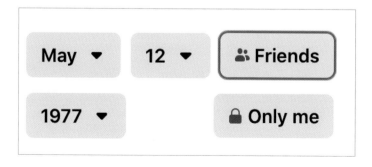

Searching for Facebook friends

You can also manually look for people to connect with on Facebook using the social network's powerful search tools.

Performing a quick search

Hot tip

Once friends start accepting your invitations, Facebook will suggest people you may know based on mutual friends, the networks you form, your imported contacts and any other information, such as details of your workplace or where you went to school or university.

1 On any Facebook screen, click the Search bar, which contains the words **Search Facebook**. Type a request

2 As you type, a list of suggestions will appear. You can select one of these if you wish

3 Otherwise, tap **Enter** on your keyboard and you will see a list of people. Look down the list and see if you recognize anyone from their image and/or location

4 If you want to connect with someone, click the **Add Friend** icon, which is to the right of their name

5 If you are not sure you have the right person, then you can investigate further. Start by hovering over their name for more details, or even click to view their profile. You may also be able to take a good look at their profile to see their photos or the friends you may have in common. You can even send them a message

Beware

You cannot send more than 1,000 friend requests at any one time. If you try to do so then Facebook will delete the earliest friend requests in favor of the ones you've just added.

Searching via the mobile app

We have not yet looked at downloading, installing and using the Facebook apps for smartphones and tablets. But you can also search for friends on these devices.

1 Tap the **Search** icon at the top of the app (it looks like a magnifying glass)

2 A search bar will appear at the top containing the words **Search Facebook**

3 Tap the name of a friend and select **See results for [search query]**

4 Go down the list and if you spot the person that you're hoping to add, tap the **Add Friend** icon to the right of their name

5 If their name does not appear in the preliminary list, simply select **See All** and follow Step 4 if this unveils the person you are searching for

Using the filters to narrow down your search

The search results are split across different categories. As well as finding people, Facebook can also let you look for words associated with Posts, Groups, Photos, and more. By searching within a category, you have access to filters.

1 When viewing the results, select **People**

2 Click **Filters** to narrow your search by inputting a city, a school/university or work

3 To only view friends of friends, click the toggle to the **On** position

Beware

Only connect with people that you genuinely know. If you want to become friends with a stranger, perhaps because they are famous or interesting, consider following them instead. We show you how to do this on page 28.

23

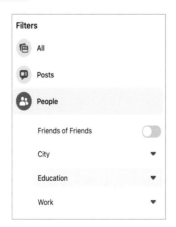

Filters	
All	
Posts	
People	
Friends of Friends	⬤
City	▾
Education	▾
Work	▾

Hot tip

If you find there is no option to add someone as a friend, it may be because their privacy settings only let them accept requests from friends of friends. If this is the case, send them a message and ask them to invite you.

Dealing with a friend request

When someone tries to connect with you, accepting or declining their request is very straightforward.

Accepting a friend request

1 When someone requests that you become their friend, a notification will appear in the bar that runs down the right-hand side of the desktop version of Facebook. It sits above your list of contacts

2 First, consider whether or not you wish to accept the request. It is a good idea to click the contact to make sure you definitely know the person but if you do want to connect, then simply select **Confirm**

Hot tip

When you receive a friend request, it will always indicate how many mutual friends you have with that person.

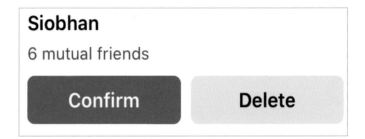

Siobhan

6 mutual friends

Confirm	Delete

Declining a friend request

1 If you do not wish to connect with the person contacting you, click **Delete**. You do not have to give a reason for declining their invitation

2 The request will be removed from your list. But don't worry. The person sending you the friend request will not be informed that you have decided not to accept it. The only way they will know is if they check your profile in the future and see that the **Add Friend** option against your name is once again available

Hot tip

Friend requests also appear on your mobile device. Look under the Notification tab of the mobile app (it looks like a bell).

Ensuring others can find you

What if you are finding that other people are still struggling to find you? It could well be, for example, that they are searching for you using a different name.

Facebook allows you to add alternative names, such as a nickname, maiden name, alternative spelling, married name, father's name, birth name, former name, and name with title.

Adding extra names to Facebook

1 Click **About** on your profile

2 Select **Details About You** from the left-hand menu

3 Click **+ Add a nickname, a birth name...**

4 Click the drop-down menu next to **Name Type** to select the kind of name you are adding

5 Write the required name in the **Name** box

6 Decide whether or not you want the name to show at the top of your profile

7 Click **Save**

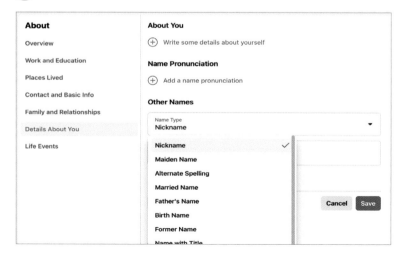

Controlling who can Friend you

Although the idea of Facebook is to forge links with other people, there will inevitably be some individuals who you would much rather avoid. Thankfully, there are three key ways of exerting some control over those you come across on Facebook. You can:

● Limit the people who can contact you to friends of friends.

● Block individuals from contacting you.

● Unfriend those you have already accepted.

Limiting who can contact you

1 Click the downward arrow in the Navigation bar at the top of the screen and select **Settings & Privacy**

2 Choose **Settings** located at the top of the menu

3 Click **Privacy** from the left-hand menu

4 You will see a section entitled **How People Find and Contact You**. The first option is **Who can send you friend requests?**. Click **Edit** next to it

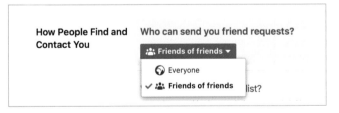

5 There are two options: Everyone and Friends of friends. Select **Friends of friends** and click **Close**. Now, only people connected with your friends on Facebook can send you a request. Everyone else will have to contact you direct and ask that you Friend them

Blocking someone

Blocking is something of an extreme measure in the world of social networking. It will prevent someone from viewing anything you post, and bar them from interacting with you.

Reasons for blocking people vary, but often it is because of abusive, bullying, sexist or racist behavior. Harassment, trolling and the sharing of sexually explicit content will also cause people to block others.

1 Click the downward arrow in the Navigation bar at the top of the screen and select **Settings & Privacy**

2 Click **Settings**

3 Select **Blocking** in the left-side menu

4 In the **Block users** section, you can type the name of a person you want to block. After doing so, click **Block**

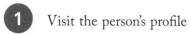

Unfriending someone

You can also decide to stop being friends with someone. The other person will not be notified.

1 Visit the person's profile

2 Click on the **Friends** icon

3 Click **Unfriend** from the menu

4 Click **Confirm** to remove

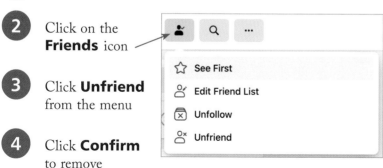

Even when you block someone, you may still see their name crop up during your use of Facebook. They can appear in posts made by mutual friends or in Groups and message conversations, for example. They won't, however, be able to interact with you directly.

Find out how to report offensive posts on page 178.

27

If someone has unfriended you you'll only find out if you go to their profile page, and there is an option to add them as a friend.

When you become friends with someone, you will automatically follow them.

For another way to unfollow people, go to page 35.

Allowing anyone to potentially follow you is only advisable if you intend to create posts that you want the world to see or read.

Following other people

Facebook advises that you only become friends with people you know. But what if you want to hook up with someone who you are not on friendly terms with – a celebrity or someone in the public eye, perhaps?

For those circumstances, look for a button on their profile called Follow. Not everyone has it because it must be activated, but for those that do:

1 Click the **three-dot** icon and select **Follow**

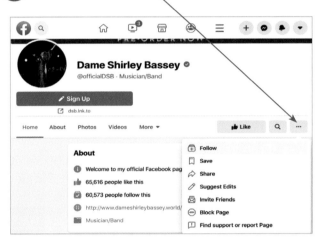

2 Then, click the three-dot icon again and click **Follow Settings**. Here, you can select how you see the posts and the types you'd like to be notified of. You can also select to **Unfollow**

Activating the Follow button on your profile
If you want everybody to be able to follow you, then:

1 Click the downward arrow in the top-right corner of Facebook, and choose **Settings & Privacy**

2 Click **Public Posts** in the left-hand menu

3 In the top section marked **Who can follow me?** click the button marked Friends, and change it to **Public**

3 Familiarizing yourself with Facebook

Facebook's News Feed is a key feature of the social network, since it gathers together any posts created by your friends.

Understanding the interface

Now that you have set up a Facebook account and begun the process of finding and adding friends, you are ready to start interacting.

There are a number of key things you can do to get the ball rolling with your account. You could:

- Read what your friends are up to.

- Write a status update or tell the world how you feel.

- Post a photograph or a video.

- Check in at your current location.

Before you do, however, it is a good idea to become familiar with the Facebook interface.

Looking at your Facebook Home screen

Your Facebook Home screen is split into various sections that run across three columns. To the left is the menu; in the middle is your News Feed; and to the right is a list of notifications including friend requests, birthdays and contacts. Much of your attention will be focused on the middle section.

Hot tip

The left-hand menu helps you navigate the various Facebook sections. It will display any Groups you join and Pages you create, while showing the apps you use, any events of interest, and items that you save.

Create Post. This section is toward the top of the middle column. You can use it to write something, and to add photos and videos and feelings to your Timeline – the place where your updates and posts are featured.

Things to do. Facebook often highlights items that it wants to bring to your attention. Here, it is showcasing its Rooms feature.

Posts. Running down the rest of this middle section are posts from friends, as well as organizations and Groups that you may decide to follow.

Sponsored posts are also placed within the News Feed, and it rapidly becomes a hive of activity. The more friends post and others respond, the more you'll find yourself returning to keep up with the latest gossip and news.

Hot tip

As well as Groups, you will encounter Pages. These are aimed at businesses, organizations, public figures and other such bodies, and they are always public and available for anyone to join by Liking. You will interact with a Page in the same way as a personal profile and posts from them will appear in your Timeline. You can start your own Page by selecting **Pages** from the left-hand menu and selecting **+ Create New Page**. Fill in the page name, category and description and build it in the same way as you would your own profile.

Using the Navigation bar to get around
You'll also find yourself using the Navigation bar at the top of the screen on many occasions. It remains constant, regardless of which page you are on.

- Clicking either the Facebook icon or Home takes you to the Home screen.

- Search Facebook lets you find friends, people and Groups.

- The TV icon takes you to Facebook Watch.

- The house icon in the middle is for Marketplace.

- The icon featuring people takes you to Groups.

- The icon shaped like two blocks is for Gaming.

- The speech bubble icon takes you to Messenger.

Searching Facebook

The Search bar at the top of the Facebook screen is a powerful tool. Most people will use it to look for potential friends but it can also find Pages, Groups, posts, photographs, events and apps.

Why not try:

● Searching for a name?

● Looking for an email address?

● Inputting a telephone number?

● Making a general search using keywords?

When you search on Facebook, your search terms are saved. The most recent are displayed in a drop-down list as you type.

Searching for a specific item

Let's look for items that reflect an interest – for example, recipes.

1 Type the required keyword(s) in the Search bar

2 Press **Enter**

3 The results will appear, split into sections such as Pages; Videos; Posts from Friends; Photos; Groups; Featured Posts; News; People; and Public Posts

4 Scroll down the screen and click on anything you like the look of

Checking your News Feed

Checking your News Feed is as simple as visiting your Facebook Home screen. Use your mouse to scroll down the screen, and stop whenever you find something interesting. There are certain things to watch out for:

- Every post contains the name of the person who created it.

- Every post tells you when it was made, either using the actual date and time, or the number of hours that have passed.

- Every post has up to three methods of interaction: **Like**, **Comment** and **Share**.

You may see posts in your News Feed from people and Groups you have not connected with. That's because a friend will have directly interacted with them in some way.

When friends continue to Like or Comment on a post, it raises the chance of you seeing it more than once.

You can stop videos from autoplaying by clicking the downward-facing arrow in the top-right corner of Facebook. Simply select Settings, click Videos in the left-hand menu, and change **Default** next to **Auto-Play Videos** to Off.

Playing videos

Some posts contain videos or images. Videos will automatically play without sound from within your News Feed.

If you want to hear a video, simply click on the audio option in the bottom-right corner and move the slider to adjust the volume.

Tailoring your News Feed

What you see in your News Feed depends to a large extent on how you use Facebook. If you interact with certain people more than others, for example, then the social network's clever algorithms will make their posts a priority.

Facebook also tracks your actions, figuring out which posts you tend to engage with the most, paying careful attention to who posted it and when, the level of interactions, and the type of content. In doing so, it aims to deliver the most relevant stories for you. But that doesn't mean you can't tweak your News Feed.

Prioritizing who you want to see first

1 Click the downward arrow to the far right of the Navigation bar. Select **Settings & Privacy**

2 Choose **News Feed Preferences**

3 In the News Feed Preferences panel, click **See First**

4 Select the star next to the people or Groups you want to prioritize

5 You can make life easier by using the panel's search engine and filtering by Friends and Pages

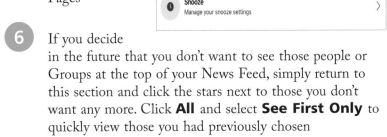

6 If you decide in the future that you don't want to see those people or Groups at the top of your News Feed, simply return to this section and click the stars next to those you don't want any more. Click **All** and select **See First Only** to quickly view those you had previously chosen

Unfollowing people

If you decide to unfollow people, you will remain friends but you just won't see their posts in your News Feed.

1 Follow the first two steps on the previous page, but this time select **Unfollow**

2 Click the blue icon next to the people and Pages whose posts you don't want to see any more

3 Click the **X** when you're done or else select the back arrow button

4 If you need to reconnect with those people at any point in the future, then select **Reconnect** in the News Feed Preferences menu. You'll see a list of people you choose to stop seeing. Clicking the **+** icon will allow you to start seeing their posts and stories again

Hot tip

You can unfollow people and Groups by visiting their profile or Page, clicking the three-dot menu and choosing the option to Unfollow.

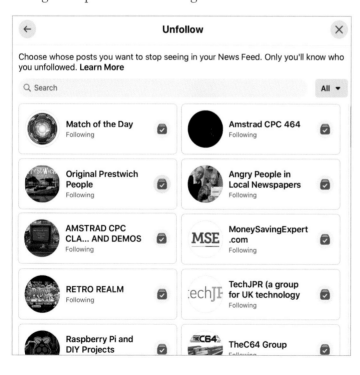

Hiding a post from your Feed

Have you come across a post you'd rather not see or a post that keeps cropping up over and over again? You can hide it from your News Feed.

1 Look for the three-dot **Menu** button in the top right-hand corner of the post, and click it

2 Select **Hide post**

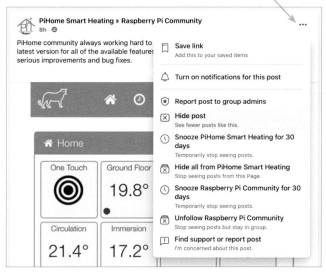

Reporting a post, image or video

If a post is offensive or you feel it breaches your privacy, you can report it:

1 Click the three-dot **Menu** button on the post

2 Select the option to **Find support or report post**

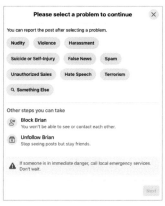

3 State why you don't like it, by selecting a problem and clicking **Next**. You can also take steps to block, unfollow or unfriend the offending poster

Commenting on a post

Facebook encourages you to respond to posts made by other people, and the ability to comment appears beneath each one. Be aware, though, that if you comment on a post that is public, it can be read by anyone online – not just those in your social circle. If you comment on a friend's post, their privacy settings regarding the post will also affect who can read it.

Writing a comment

1 Underneath a post, you will see a section button inviting you to **Write a comment...** (you may have to click the **Comment** option first). Click this box when you want to reply to something you have read, seen or watched

2 Compose your message in the text box and press **Enter** on your keyboard to post it

3 Your comment will appear beneath the post for others to read. To get involved in a conversation, you can click **Reply** beneath anyone else's comment. Comments can be edited and deleted, and you are also free to write as many as you wish

Posting a sticker

1 Believe a picture paints a thousand words? Then use a sticker. Click the **square smiley face** in the Comment text box

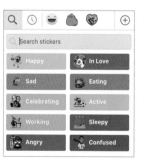

2 Look through the categories, from Happy to Confused, and choose a sticker. Click **+** if you want to look through the Sticker Store. These are packs of new stickers, many of which are free. Find a sticker you like? Select it to post

Hot tip

You can mention (or "tag") a person in a post. Just type their name and select them from a list. They will be notified that you have tagged them. See page 139 for more on this.

Don't forget

If you like stickers, keep checking the Sticker Store since there are sometimes updates surrounding holidays and movie releases.

Hot tip

As well as selecting a sticker, you can also choose and send a GIF in Facebook comments. Click the GIF button in the Comment text box.

Don't forget

Much of the fun of Facebook is interacting with others and seeing people react to you, so don't be afraid to get stuck in.

Reacting to a post

Reading posts is all well and good, but you're bound to have a burning desire to react to something a friend or Group has written, uploaded or created. It used to be that Facebook only allowed you to Like a post, but now there is a range of six other reactive emotions:

Expressing a reaction to someone's post

1 Beneath a post you will see an option called **Like**. You can simply click this if you do indeed like something you see

2 Alternatively, hover your mouse over **Like** without clicking it, and more reactions will appear. Choose between **Love**, **Care**, **Haha**, **Wow**, **Sad** and **Angry**, depending on how the post makes you feel

3 Your name will appear alongside your reaction within the post. You will also be able to see if and how others have reacted to the post too

4 An entry will appear on your Timeline to say you have reacted to a post, and the person who created it will also be notified of your interaction

5 If you change your mind or if you've clicked the wrong reaction, go back and select something different

6 To remove a reaction entirely, just click the one you've currently selected

4 Creating your first Facebook posts

This chapter explains how you can create your own posts, bring them to the attention of others, and make use of photos and videos.

Creating a written post

Although reading, seeing and reacting to what others are posting is entertaining enough, very soon you will want to spark your own conversations. You do this by creating a post, and the simplest of these involves writing a few words about what you are up to, or getting something off your chest.

1 Go to the Homepage or your Timeline

2 At the top of the second column, you will see a box containing the words **What's on your mind?**

3 Click the box, and a window will appear

4 You can now write anything you wish in this box

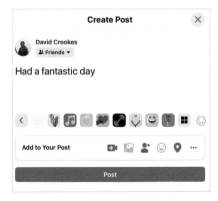

5 Click the drop-down menu labeled **Friends**. Select who should see your post: anyone, just friends, or a select few. See pages 26-27 for more details

6 When you are finished, click **Post**

Expressing your feelings

No – we're not about to sit you down on the couch and ask you to express your inner thoughts. Instead, we're going to show you how you can share your current mood or better get across what you are currently doing or want to do.

Beware

If you are using this feature to flag up a book you are reading, or a movie or TV show you are watching, the activity will also be entered on your About page.

1 Click the icon for **Feeling/Activity** within the **Create Post** box. Now, click it again

2 You will see two categories: **Feelings** and **Activities**

3 Select the category you want to use and scroll down the list of icons. Feelings include happy, loved and sad. Activities include celebrating, eating and watching

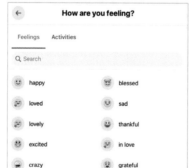

4 The feeling or activity will then appear within your post. You can write something in relation to it if you wish

5 When you are finished, click **Post**

6 Your friends will be able to view this extra piece of information within your post

Checking in to a location

If you want to include a location in your post, you can "check in". Facebook will look for an identifiable place.

Beware

Many security experts urge caution when using this feature since it could reveal when you're not at home or, if you are, where you live.

1 In the **Create Post** box, click the icon for **Check in**

2 A drop-down list will suggest potential locations. If your location is there, click it

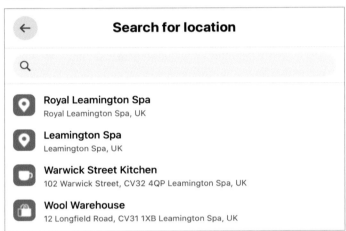

← **Search for location**

🔍

📍 **Royal Leamington Spa**
Royal Leamington Spa, UK

📍 **Leamington Spa**
Leamington Spa, UK

☕ **Warwick Street Kitchen**
102 Warwick Street, CV32 4QP Leamington Spa, UK

🛍 **Wool Warehouse**
12 Longfield Road, CV31 1XB Leamington Spa, UK

3 If it is not listed, you can simply write your current location in the text box. More suggestions will be made as you type

4 You can now write something (or leave it blank) and select **Post** when you have finished. Your post will be accompanied by a map pinpointing your location for others to see

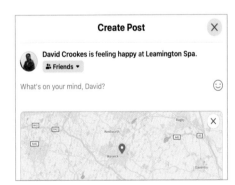

Create Post ✕

David Crookes is feeling happy at Leamington Spa.
👥 Friends ▼

What's on your mind, David? ☺

42

Tagging your friends in posts

A popular method of connecting with people who are already friends with you is to tag them in your posts. Doing this produces a link to their profile, which anyone who sees it is able to view. Your post may also appear on your friend's Timeline, widening the number of people who will see it.

1 Create a post then click the three-dot menu in the **Add to Your Post** section

2 Select the **Tag Friends** option

Any friends you tag will be notified of your action. It can be worthwhile asking them whether they mind you tagging them before you do it.

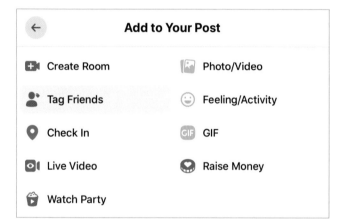

← **Add to Your Post**

- Create Room
- Tag Friends
- Check In
- Live Video
- Watch Party
- Photo/Video
- Feeling/Activity
- GIF
- Raise Money

3 Search for a friend by either scrolling down the list or entering their name in the Search bar that appears. You can add more than one friend and, as you click their names, they appear in a box named **Tagged**

4 Click **Done** and their name will appear in the **Create Post** box

5 Write something, and click **Post** when you have finished

6 A clickable link bearing their name will appear in your post when it becomes viewable on Facebook

Selecting who sees your posts

Facebook allows you to control who is able to see your posts. You can do this on a post-by-post basis. What you choose is very much down to you and the content that you are looking to share.

Beware

The setting you choose remains in place for all subsequent posts until you change it again.

Don't forget

If you tag someone in a post, they will be able to control how the post will appear on their Timeline.

Hot tip

Custom lists let you post updates for a specific group of people such as a handful of close friends or family members. Select **Friend Lists** from Facebook's left-hand menu and click **+ Create List**. Give the list a title and begin adding names, clicking **Create** when you've finished. Now you can choose **Custom** when selecting who can see your post – just enter the name of the list in the **Share with** box.

1 In the **Create Post** box, click the icon for **Friends**

👥 Friends ▾

2 You will see a number of options. After writing a post, you can:

- **Make it Public**. This allows anyone to see what you have posted, whether or not they are using Facebook.

- **Allow your friends to see it**. Those you have added as a friend will see the post in their News Feeds.

- **Exclude some friends from seeing it**. This will stop it from appearing in certain friends' News Feeds.

- **Let specific friends see it**. Only those on your list will read or see your posts.

- **Keep it to yourself**. It'll be solely for your eyes.

3 You can also decide whether you wish to post to any custom lists that you create

4 If you decide to limit your post to certain friends, then you'll be shown a list of your connections. Add or remove people who you do and don't want to see your post, before clicking **Save Changes**

5 Click **Post** to send it on its way

Enhancing your posts

If you want to make your posts more eye-catching, there are three good ways of doing this: changing the background color of your post, adding stickers or using an emoji.

Changing the background

1 Click on the **Create Post** box and click the **Aa** icon

2 This shows a series of colored squares, each corresponding to a different background

3 Click the one you like. If you change your mind and want a plain background again, select the white square

Adding an emoji

1 Click on the **Create Post** box and click the **Aa** icon

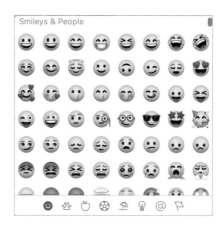

2 Click the smiley face icon

3 You will see lots of emojis. Choose a category at the bottom of the box and select the one you want

Hot tip

Select **Check in** after choosing an image or video if you want to add a location to it.

Posting a photo or video

As well as posting text, you are also able to post photos and videos. Uploading images and videos is a great way of sharing your day-to-day activities. You can post media that you own yourself, or media that you find online.

Posting your own photographs and videos

1 When you are ready to post a photo or video, click the **Photo/Video** icon in the **Create Post** box

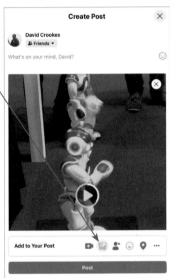

2 Browse your computer for the photograph or video you want to upload

3 To add more photos, hover over the video you've attached to the **Create Post** box and click **Add Photos/Videos**. Then, browse your computer for more images or videos

4 You can write some words about the photo or video. Click **Post** to upload

Identifying friends in a photograph
If you want to identify who is in the photograph with you:

1 Click the image within the **Create Post** box before you upload it

2 Click **Edit**

3 Click **Tag photo** then click on the image and it will allow you to identify the people who are in it

Posting photos you find online

When surfing the web, you are bound to come across interesting and funny photographs. You may wish to share these with your friends on Facebook. Doing so is very easy:

1 Right-click a photograph you like on a web page

2 Look for an option that allows you to copy an image address. This varies from computer to computer and browser to browser, but the choices can include Copy Image Address, Copy Image Location or Copy Image URL, or even a straightforward Copy

3 Right-click in the **Create Post** box on Facebook, and select **Paste**. The image will now appear

4 Write some accompanying text, and click **Post**

Hot tip

You can also copy a web address generated by YouTube after pressing Share, and manually paste it into a post.

Posting a video you find online

Many video websites allow you to share their content on social media. YouTube, for example, has a dedicated Share button that produces a link you can use.

1 Visit **youtube.com** and look for a video

2 Click the **Share** button beneath it

3 Select the icon for Facebook, and a Post window will open. The video will be automatically included

4 Write your message, and click **Post to Facebook**

Hot tip

If you want to share a specific point in a video, YouTube has an option that lets you choose a start time. You'll see it under the web address in YouTube's Share box.

Sharing someone else's post

You will often come across a post that you would like to share with others. Luckily, every post comes with a Share option, which allows you to share links with anybody you wish. You won't, however, be able to widely share images, videos or status updates by a friend if their privacy settings restrict their posts to a specific audience. Here is how to share posts:

1 Click the option for **Share** underneath a post

2 Select how you want to share it. You can:

- **Share Now (Friends).** This instantly shares the post and does not give you an opportunity to comment on it.

- **Share to News Feed.** You will have the option to write something too.

- **Share to Your Story (Custom).** Images and videos can be shared to a Facebook Story where they will remain for 24 hours.

- **Send in Messenger.** Posts can be sent direct and privately to one person via Facebook Messenger (see Chapter 8).

- **Share to a Group.** If you are a Group member, you can share a post to it.

- **Share on a Friend's Timeline.** Use if you want to bring it to someone's attention publicly.

3 If you're sharing to a Group, you'll be asked to specify which Group you're sharing to by clicking **Share**. We cover Groups in Chapter 6

4 If clicking **Share on a Friend's Timeline**, write the name of your friend in the window that appears

Enhance your shared post when sharing to your News Feed by adding a location, tagging others, using emojis or choosing a picture to indicate how you feel. The options appear at the bottom of the Share window.

Editing your posts

When you create a post, it is not set in stone. Sometimes you'll look at it and spot a mistake, or you'll wish you hadn't put it up. Facebook allows for such eventualities by letting you edit and even delete posts. You can also change the date of the post and hide it from your Timeline.

Making changes to a post

1 To edit a post, click the three-dot **Menu** button in the top-right corner and select **Edit post**

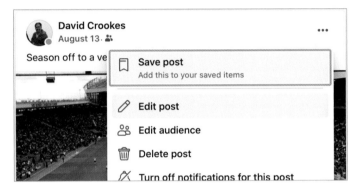

2 The post will appear in a new window, allowing you to change the text, add or remove images and videos, tag people, include an emoji, and check in. You can also change who can see your post and remove the location

3 Click **Save** when you have finished editing

Changing the date

1 If you want to alter the date of your post, click the downward arrow and select **Change Date**. Use the drop-down options to alter the year, month and day

2 Click **Time** to change the time

3 Click **Save**

Hot tip

Simply click **Delete** from the drop-down menu and confirm to remove an unwanted post.

Hot tip

If you don't want a post to appear on your Timeline, select **Hide from Timeline**. The post will still appear in your friends' News Feeds, unless you delete it altogether.

Hot tip

Turning off notifications for a post means Facebook won't let you know if someone responds to it.

Creating Facebook Stories

As well as posting content to your Timeline and allowing others to see it in their News Feed, you can share your images, videos or text as a Story. Often based around a particular theme and, in effect, acting like a second News Feed, content posted to a Story can be viewed for 24 hours before disappearing.

1 Tap **Create a Story**, which you will find at the top of your News Feed

2 Decide if you are going to **Create a Photo Story** or **Create a Text Story**

Creating a Photo Story

1 Find an image on your device and click **Choose**

2 Once it is in Facebook's Preview window, you can click the image and edit it. Use the slider to crop the image, and the **Rotate** button to flip the image by 90 degrees at a time. You can also click and drag the image so that it's neatly positioned within the viewing window

Hot tip

You can also share posts to your Story. Click **Share** below a post in your News Feed and you will see an option called **Share to Your Story** (you will not see this option if the privacy settings for that post do not allow sharing).

Hot tip

Remove content from your Story by opening it and clicking **...** in the top-right corner. Now, click **Delete**.

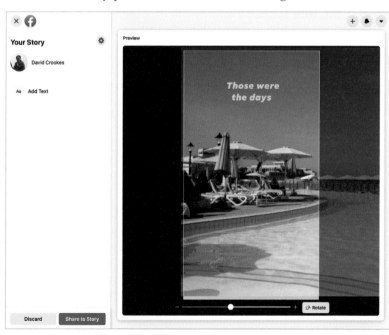

3 Click **Add Text** and you can insert text over the image. There are font and color options and, once you've written your words, you can drag them into position

4 Decide who should see your Story by clicking the **Settings** cog and choosing between **Public**, **Friends** and **Custom**. The latter lets you click and select specific friends. When you're finished, click **Done**

5 Click **Share to Story**

Creating a Text Story

Text Stories can give a Story additional context, be used to express an opinion or put to use in any way you wish.

1 Type your words in the box that says **Start typing** and they will appear in the Preview window

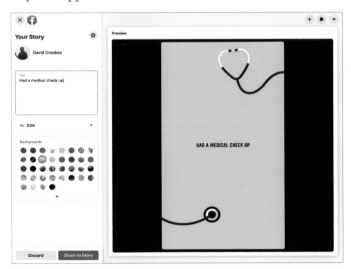

2 Select a font from the drop-down menu and a background

3 See Step 4 above and click **Share to Story**

Hot tip

Your Story can be seen at the top of the News Feed. You can click your own Story to view it and, if you want to add extra content, click **+** next to your Story's name.

51

Don't forget

When you're creating a Story, bear the Facebook mobile apps in mind because they offer more options (see pages 66-67).

Hot tip

Use the Filter option when searching to narrow down the amount of information you can see. These let you filter by posts, activity and photos you're tagged in; items hidden from the Timeline; Likes and Reactions; and more.

Viewing your activity log

Everything that you post and share is logged by Facebook, but you are able to see a list of your activities and manage it.

1 Click the downward arrow in the top-right corner of any Facebook Page

2 Select **Settings & Privacy**

3 Click **Activity Log**

← **Settings & Privacy**

⚙ Settings

🔐 Privacy Checkup

🔒 Privacy Shortcuts

☰ Activity Log

🖥 News Feed Preferences

🌐 Language

4 Look down the list in the column. You can see anything you have archived or trashed, and review your Timeline, Photos and Tags

5 Look under the **Today** heading and you will see any posts you've liked, your search terms and comments

6 Continue to scroll to see yesterday and previous days

7 Any entry can be clicked to view. When you do, some will show a three-dot **Menu** button. Click this and you will be able to **Delete** an entry or **Unlike** a Like

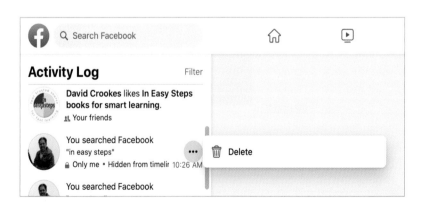

5 Starting to use the Facebook app

As well as accessing Facebook via a browser on your computer, you can also check your News Feed, search for friends, and engage with others using an app on a mobile device. This is great for keeping in touch with others, no matter where you may be.

Downloading the Facebook app

You can also visit **facebook.com** in any browser (such as Safari or Chrome) on any mobile device.

So far, we have looked at accessing Facebook via a browser on a computer. This, however, is only one way of enjoying the services that the social network provides.

More than half of all users access the service only on a mobile device. That means they are using their smartphones and tablet computers as the sole method of creating posts, checking their News Feeds, enjoying videos, and so much more.

Since more than 80 percent of us are now said to own a smartphone or tablet, there's a good chance that you will want to use Facebook on a mobile device too. Just like the website, there is no charge for doing this. You can open a browser on your phone and visit **facebook.com** to access a website specifically tailored for mobile use, or you can download a dedicated app.

Downloading the Facebook app for Apple iOS
The app is available for Apple's iOS operating system, which means it can be downloaded and installed for the iPhone, iPod touch and iPad.

1 Open the App Store on your iOS device by tapping its icon on your Home screen

2 In the Search bar at the top of the screen, type **Facebook** and tap **Search**

3 It should appear as the first search result. You can tap the entry to read more about it if you wish but to download it, tap **Get**

4 Enter your Apple ID password, and the app will download to your device

5 Tap **Open** to launch it. In future, look for the icon on your Home screen and tap that

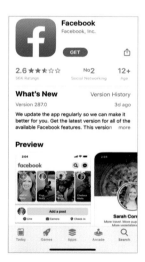

Downloading the Facebook app for Android

Android is currently the most popular mobile operating system, so it will come as no surprise to learn that you download Facebook to any smartphone or tablet that runs it.

1 Open the Play Store app on your Android device by tapping the icon on your phone or tablet's Home screen

2 In the Search bar at the top of the screen, type **Facebook** and tap the magnifying glass icon

3 If you want to immediately install Facebook, tap the **Install** button in the search result for the social network. You can also tap **More Info** and read details about it. There is an **Install** button on that page too

4 As long as you are logged in to Google on your device, it will install

5 Go to your Home screen by tapping the on-screen **Home** button. Look for and tap the Facebook icon in the applications tray of your device to open it

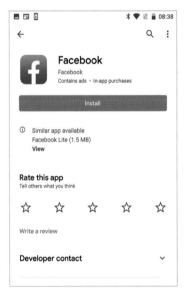

There is also a Facebook app available for Amazon's Kindle Fire tablets. Find it at https://www.amazon.com/Facebook/dp/B0094BB4TW

55

Logging in to the Facebook app

With the app installed on your device, it is time to log in.

1 Open the mobile app for the first time, and you will be asked to log in using the email address or phone number that you always use to access your account

2 If you have forgotten your password, simply tap **Forgotten password?** and it will seek to verify your identity before allowing you to input a new one

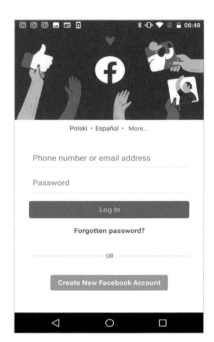

3 You will be asked if you wish to save your login details on your device so that you do not always have to keep entering it whenever you open the app

4 Facebook will also ask whether or not you want to allow it to access your location. This, it says, allows certain features to work properly

Logging out of the Facebook app

1 If you need to log out of the app, tap the **Menu** button (this looks like three horizontal lines and you will find it in the bottom-right corner of the iOS Facebook app and in the top-right corner of the Android app)

2 Scroll to the very bottom of this page and you will see an option to **Log Out**. Simply tap this. You'll need to re-input your username and password next time you try to access the Facebook app

Understanding the interface

When you start using Facebook on your mobile device, whether a smartphone or tablet, it will default to your News Feed. This allows you catch up with the latest gossip, news and videos when you're on the move. But what can you see on the screen? Here are some of the basics:

Pull down on the screen when viewing the News Feed to refresh it.

Perform searches. Find various things on Facebook.

Write a post. Create text and photo/video posts.

Rooms and Stories. Get involved in a video chat or create a visual-themed feed.

Various posts from others. Use your finger to scroll down this screen and view posts created by others. Leave a reaction, make a comment or share any posts you enjoy.

Explore other areas of Facebook. These icons take you to other sections and features of the social network.

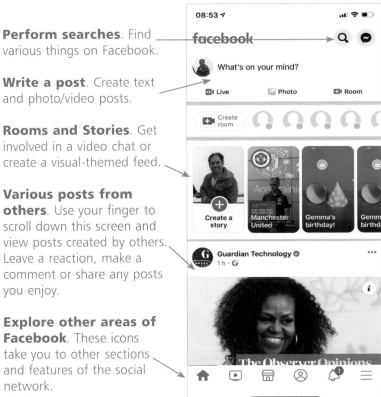

Other versions

We have pictured the iOS version above, but other versions differ ever so slightly.

The Android version, for example, has some of its key features placed on the screen in a slightly different order.

This is due to the positioning of the Android buttons at the bottom of the screen.

Viewing your own profile

As we've just seen, the Facebook app will take you direct to your News Feed by default. But you can view your own profile too.

1   Tap the **Menu** icon. You will see this in the bottom right-hand corner of the iOS app and in the top right-hand corner of the Android app

2   Select **View your profile**

Looking at your profile on iOS

Edit the profile. Tap this icon and you can edit your profile image, the cover photo, your bio, details, hobbies, links and add featured Stories, photos or videos.

Profile image. Your current image will be positioned at the top of the profile page. You can tap the Camera icon to change it. You can also add a frame around the image.

Add Story. Here, you can create a Story from scratch or add to an existing one.

See Your About Info. Check the details you've added about yourself and edit them.

Friends. You'll see how many friends you have connected with. You can also tap Find Friends and see suggested people you may know.

More. As well as icons for Home, Watch, Marketplace, Profile and Notifications, you can tap More for a large menu of options.

Looking at your profile on Android

Search your posts. A Search bar is located at the top of your profile page.

Profile image. The image you are currently using will be located here, beneath your cover image. Both can be edited by tapping the Camera icon.

Create a Story/Add to Story. Tap here to begin a Story or add to an existing one.

About info. Any information you've inputted about yourself will be in this editable section.

Edit Public Details. You can make amends to your bio.

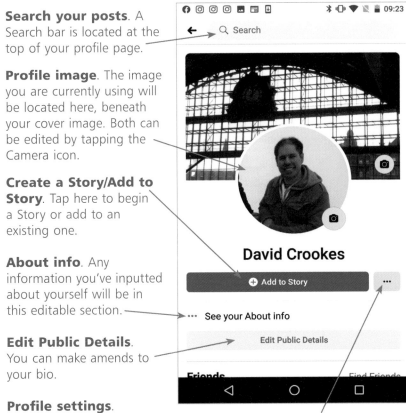

Profile settings. Tap here to edit your profile, see your activity log, review your Timeline, and more.

Other important information on your profile

As you continue to scroll down the screen, you will see a few other sections. You will be able to:

- View any photos you have posted or uploaded.

- Review the personal information held on your profile.

- See how many friends you have, check their profiles and check out how many new posts they have created.

- View, edit and even delete your own posts.

Finding friends and more

You can use the search engine within the app to quickly look for friends. This search engine can also be used to find posts, videos, Pages, photos, places, Groups, apps and events, just as it can on the computer version of Facebook.

Hot tip

If you are looking for a post you can tap **Filter**, which will help narrow down the search by date, person posting and tags.

1 Tap the Search bar at the top of the screen

2 Begin typing your search term

3 As you type, Facebook will make suggestions. You can stop typing at any time and tap one of those suggestions

4 You can also continue typing and tap **Search** or **See results for** when you are finished

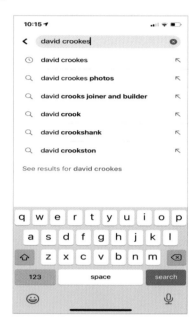

5 The results page will be displayed. If you are looking for a friend, you may find them by tapping the **People** button at the top of the screen. You can also tap the tabs for other categories if you are looking for something other than a person, such as a post

6 When you have found someone you wish to add, you can tap the icon next to their name. If you want to find out more about them, however, to be sure you have the correct person, tap their name

7 You will be taken to their profile page. Tap **Add Friend** and a friend request will be sent to the person. Now, sit back and wait for them to agree

Checking friend requests

When people try to become friends with you on Facebook, their requests appear within the app. You can accept or decline them.

1 Tap the Notifications button at the top or the of the screen, depending on which smartphone operating system you are using

2 Look under the section marked **Friend requests** for any entries

3 If people are trying to contact you, there will be two options next to their photo and name: **Confirm** and **Delete**

4 If you wish to accept a person as a friend, tap **Confirm** to add them

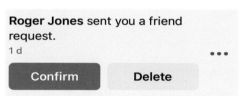

5 If you do not want to accept a request, tap **Delete**. The person will be removed from the list and the request will be denied

Checking Facebook's friend recommendations
Facebook will look for any mutual friends you have and promote them as potential people you may want to add.

1 Look under the section marked **People You May Know**

2 If there is a list of names, you'll be told how many mutual friends you share with each person

3 Decide whether to send them a request to connect. If you'd like to connect, tap **Add Friend**

Hot tip

If you receive an unwanted friend notification, tap the three-dot **Menu** button next to the request and either remove the notification or report it.

Accessing your notifications

When somebody adds something to Facebook that you are likely to be interested in, you will get a notification. This could indicate:

- **A mention**: Your name may be included in somebody's post.

- **A reaction**: A comment on a post you're involved with.

- **Something new on a Page/Group you're following**: You'll be kept informed of new posts, photos and videos.

- **A new event**: Events added by someone you are following.

- **A shared link**: Links posted to Pages and Groups you follow.

1 On a smartphone or tablet, tap the Bell icon

2 Tap any notification to view it in full

The Lowry added a new event near you: Breakin' Convention 2017 UK Tour: Salford.
Friday at 15:26

3 Read notifications will turn from blue to white

Allowing and disallowing push notifications

To be kept informed of Facebook notifications when you are not using the app, allow alerts or messages to be sent to your device.

1 For Android: Go to the **Settings** app on your device

2 Go to **Applications** and navigate to **Apps > Facebook > Notifications**

3 Use the top button to turn notifications on or off

1 For iOS: Go to the **Settings** app

2 Tap **Notifications** and then tap **Facebook**

3 Use the button next to **Allow Notifications** to turn the notifications on and off

When deciding whether to activate notifications on Android, decide if you want them to show without a sound or vibration. You can also allow them to appear when **Do Not Disturb** is turned on.

On iOS, as well as turning notifications on and off, you can also indicate how you would like them to appear and whether or not you want them to make a sound.

Adjusting your notifications

To prevent you being bombarded by notifications, you can decide on the kind of alerts that you want to receive on your device.

1 Tap the **Menu** icon within the Facebook app

2 Tap **Settings & Privacy** and select **Settings**

3 Scroll down the screen to the **Notifications** section

4 Tap **Notification settings**

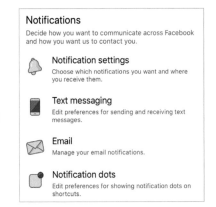

5 Decide which notifications you wish to receive. They include birthday alerts, comments, updates from friends and Group posts

6 When you tap on a notification type, you can decide where you want to receive them. Push means you'll receive an alert on your phone but you can also have them sent via email or SMS messaging

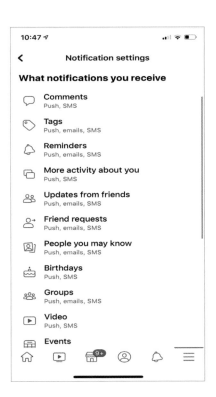

Creating a post via the app

You can create posts on both your computer (see page 40) and on the app. As well as writing a text-based post, you can upload a photo or video, check in, express a feeling or activity, tag friends, and even create a live video.

All of Facebook's cross-platform apps work in much the same way.

Don't forget

You can determine who should see your post by clicking **Friends** in the status update box.

64

Hot tip

You can use a post to let others know where you are by tapping **Check in**. You will be shown a list of locations or you can search manually. Tap a location to add it. See page 68 for the settings needed to activate this feature if you find it is not working for you.

1 Tap the status update box

2 Select the type of post you wish to create from the menu that appears beneath the main text-entry window

3 If you simply want to write a text-based post, tap **What's on your mind?** in order to call up the on-screen keyboard

4 You can add photos and videos to your post, check in, or choose a feeling or activity by selecting one of the icons at the bottom of the text window. There's an option to change the background color too

> What's on your mind?
>
> Live   Photo   Room

> 10:53
>
> ✕   **Create post**   Post
>
> David Crookes
> Friends ▾   + Album ▾
>
> What's on your mind?

> Create room
> Photo/Video
> Tag friends
> Feeling/Activity
> Check in
> GIF

5 When you have completed your status update, tap **Post** in the top right-hand corner. It will now be posted to your Timeline, where it can be read by other people in their News Feeds

Adding photos and videos

Your smartphone or tablet will be packed with images and videos. You can share any of these in your posts, or take a fresh photo or video using your device's camera.

Using an existing image

1 Either tap **Photo** in the status update box or tap the status update box and select **Photo/Video**

2 In both cases, you will be shown all of the images and videos that are saved on your device. Scroll down and select one or more

3 Tap **Done** and the image(s) will be added to a post

4 Write a message and, when complete, tap **Post**

Using a simple, fresh image or video

1 Follow Step 1 above but tap the Camera icon in the top-right corner of the screen. Allow access to your device's camera if you have not already done so

2 Your device's camera will be activated. Tap the large circular button at the bottom of the screen to snap an image or record some video (you will see options for an image or video below the button). If recording video, pressing the button again will stop filming

3 Tap **Next** in iOS or **Done** in Android to place your taken image or video into a post

4 Write a message, and tap **Post** when you're finished

Hot tip

You will also notice a Camera icon in the top left-hand corner of your app's News Feed. This can produce snazzy images and videos. We look at this in greater detail in Chapter 10.

Hot tip

If you start to create a post, then decide you want to continue it later, tap the backward-facing arrow in Android, or **X** in iOS, and choose **Save as Draft**. The next time you attempt to write a status update, your previous message will appear again.

Welcome to the
Facebook camera

This feature requires
camera access
In iPhone settings, tap Facebook and
turn on Camera

Not Now   Open Settings

BOOMERANG   NORMAL   VIDEO

Creating Facebook Stories on the app

Hot tip

Your Story can be kept on your profile by launching it and tapping **Feature** in the bottom-right corner.

You can use the website version of Facebook to create a Story, and we explain how on pages 50-51. You can, however, also use the app to create Stories, and it's actually preferable because you will have access to more features. You'll find it easy to update your Story when you're out and about too.

Creating an image-based Story

1 Tap **Create a story**

2 You will now see images from your Camera Roll. Tap an image to select it. If you want to choose more than one image, tap **Select multiple**, tap the ones you want and tap **Next**

3 A number of options are available, and we cover a number of them and how they work on pages 140-142. You can add stickers or text, draw on the image, use effects and tag people. These options run down the right side of the screen although a selection of stickers is also presented toward the bottom. You can swipe left and right to view them all

4 You can also tap the **Animate** tool when creating a Story using the iOS Facebook app. This adds interesting effects to your image such as panning, zooming in and out or giving the appearance that it's bouncing

5 Images can be retained by tapping **Save**

6 Tap **Privacy** to determine who should see your Story

7 When ready to use the image (including the edits) in your Story, tap **Share to Story**. It will appear at the top of your News Feed and be viewable by those you have allowed

Creating or adding to a Story using different elements

1 Tap **Create a story** or, if you have started a Story, tap **Your Story**, tap the bottom-left arrow and select **Add to Story**

2 You'll find options at the top of the screen, including one for **Text** (see page 51 for more information about Text Stories)

3 Tap **Music** to browse songs, tapping the Play icon to listen. Some are labeled with lyrics so select those to have the words displayed. Tap a song to use it. You can also make edits: change the background color, add a sticker, change the font, or draw

4 **Boomerang** lets you create a short animation. Find something moving, take a video, and it will repeatedly play forward and back. Edit using the functions detailed on page 66 (Animate is unavailable)

5 **Mood** allows you to add a GIF to your Story

6 **Selfie** lets you take a photo via the front-facing camera

7 **Poll** lets you tap **Ask a question** to replace it with your own and tap **Yes** and **No** to change the potential answers. Tap **Next** for some editing functions

8 When you are ready, tap **Share to Story**

Hot tip

After 24 hours, your Stories aren't viewable by your selected audience but they will be available in your archive. Tap your profile image, tap the three-dot **Menu** button, and you can select **Story Archive** to see them.

Don't forget

You can see who has viewed your Story by opening it and looking in the bottom-left corner.

Altering the app permissions

Over time, Facebook will seek to access various components of your device. You can review these and stop Facebook from accessing them.

Android

Beware

Turning off some of the permissions can affect the smooth running of Facebook. Turning off access to the camera, for example, will prevent you taking new photos and videos via the app.

1 Go to your device's **Settings** app, scroll down and select **Apps & notifications**. Then, tap **App info**

2 Select **Facebook**

3 Tap **Permissions** and review the permissions Facebook has been granted, using the sliders to turn off any you are not happy with

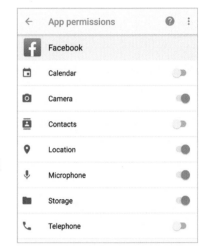

Don't forget

You can use a post to let others know where you are by using **Check in**. But you will need to turn **Location** on in the settings shown here. You must also allow your device to access your location. Go to your device's **Settings** app and, in Android, navigate to **Security & Location** > **Location** (go to **Privacy** > **Location Services** in iOS). Turn the slider **On**.

iOS

1 Go to the **Settings** app, scroll quite far down the list, and select **Facebook**

2 In the **Allow Facebook To Access** section you can now use the sliders to turn off any permissions that you do not want Facebook to have

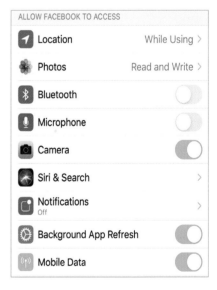

6 Working with Groups

If you have a particular interest, then you may find a Facebook Group for like-minded people. If there isn't, then you may want to set one up yourself. Facebook Groups allow you to discuss your favorite topics with others; share files, photos and videos; and foster a strong community. Facebook is also giving them greater prominence in a bid to bring the world closer together.

Joining a Facebook Group

Facebook Groups offer a wonderful way of bringing together people with a common interest. They allow members to share posts, photos, videos and documents, and they can also be made private. You can use them for:

- Organizing a party or a special occasion.

- Discussing interesting topics, ranging from photography and politics to gardening and gaming.

- Working together on a project or in the community.

- Buying and selling specific items, and much, much more.

Finding and joining a Group
It is easy to explore the different Groups that exist, and join them.

1 Click **Groups** in the left-hand menu on your computer

2 Click **Discover** and you'll be shown Group suggestions, Groups your friends are in, popular Groups in your area and a list of Group categories. If your friends are involved with a Group, their profile image will be displayed

3 To immediately request access, click **Join Group**. Otherwise, click its name to see a description and then opt to join

4 Many Groups are private so you won't always see posts, photos and other content from the Group until your join request is accepted by the Group's administrators

Engaging with a Group

Whether you have joined a public or closed Group, you are able to engage with the other members and even send invites to others.

Creating a post

You can write a post, upload a photo or video, express your feeling about an activity, check in and tag friends, just as you can when writing a post that you want to appear on your own Timeline.

If a Group has rules, you must abide by them or you risk being asked to leave. Rules are often available to view when you start writing a post.

1 Visit the Group that you wish to engage with

2 Click **What's on your mind.../Write something...** (depending on whether you're accessing Facebook on the website or via a mobile device) to create your post

3 Ensuring the name of the Group is shown, compose your post and, when finished, click **Post**

Commenting on other members' posts

When scrolling through the posts created by members, you may want to Like or Share a post. You may also want to leave a comment. You do this in the same way that you would with any post you come across (see page 37).

Using a mobile device

Navigate to the Group that you wish to engage with by tapping the three-bar **Menu** button in the app and selecting **Groups**. You can discover Groups by pressing the **Discover** button and you can scroll through a Group in the same way as you would scroll through your News Feed, liking, sharing and commenting on posts that interest you. See page 57 for more details.

Sending and receiving invitations

If you know a Facebook user who may like to become a member of a Group that you have joined, you can send them an invite.

Don't forget

If you invite people to join a closed Group, the administrator may have to grant approval before they are accepted.

1 Locate the **+ Invite** button on a Group page   `+ Invite`

2 Enter their names

3 Click **Invite**. If an invitation needs approval, the invitee will be able to preview the Group. They will ultimately decide if they wish to join or not

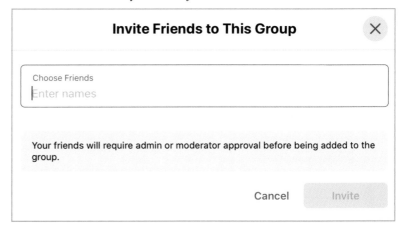

Invite Friends to This Group ✕

Choose Friends
Enter names

Your friends will require admin or moderator approval before being added to the group.

Cancel   Invite

Hot tip

Facebook will also suggest Groups for you to join based on those your friends are members of, and any pages you have liked.

Receiving an invite

When you send an invite to someone, they have the option of joining or declining. You can also be invited to join a Group.

1 Anyone invited to join a Group is sent a notification

2 They can then decide whether to **Join** or **Decline**

3 Until a Group is joined, it won't be possible to post or comment on other people's posts in that Group but it will be possible to preview the Group and see posts. This allows users to get a feel for a Group and make an informed decision before formally joining

Altering your notifications

By default, you will not receive a notification from a Group every time somebody posts to it. Instead, you will be notified of the highlights, and this includes suggested posts and any posts that are made by friends. You can alter the notification settings, however, tailoring them to best suit you.

1 Visit the Group that you want to alter the notifications for

2 Click the three-dot **Menu** button and select the option called **Manage Notifications**

3 Selecting **All Posts** will ensure you get a notification every time a member creates a post in the Group

4 Selecting **Highlights** will only show posts from your friends and suggested posts

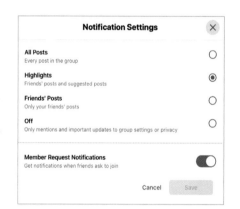

5 Selecting **Friends' Posts** will notify you only when a friend posts

6 Selecting **Off** deactivates the notifications for that particular Group. You will see and receive notifications of replies to any posts you create in the Group, however, and you will also continue to receive notifications from both other Groups and sections of Facebook

7 You can also be notified when friends join a Group. This is on by default but can be turned off by flicking the switch next to **Member Request Notifications**

8 Click **Save**

Creating a Group poll

Setting up a poll lets you gauge the opinion of other members in a Group. If the Group is about a particular genre of music, for instance, you could ask people to choose from a selection of bands. Or, if the Group concerns a birthday party, Group members could vote on the most suitable venue.

Hot tip

Only Group members can vote in polls created within Groups.

1 Go to a Group and click the three-dot **More** button in the Create Post box

2 Select **Poll**

3 Type your question where it says **Write Something**

4 Type your first poll answer in the **Option 1** box then do the same in the next two option boxes

5 For more than three options, click **+ Add option** to show an extra box

6 Click **Poll options** and you can determine if others can add their own options or whether people can choose multiple answers

7 To draw specific people to your poll, click the **Tag** icon and input their names when prompted

8 Click **Post**

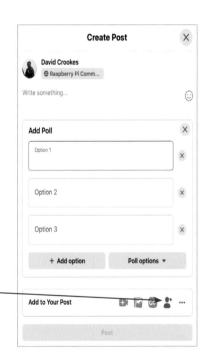

Creating a Group document

Writing a standard post will suffice most of the time, but you may want to collaborate with Group members on a document. Facebook lets you create a document that others can read and edit.

1 Go to a Group and click the three-dot **More** button in the Create Post box

2 Select **Create Doc**

3 A document will appear. Click **Title** to alter its name

4 Click **Write something...** and begin typing

5 Click the **+** icon and select **Photo** to use an image. Find a picture, and click **Upload New Photo**

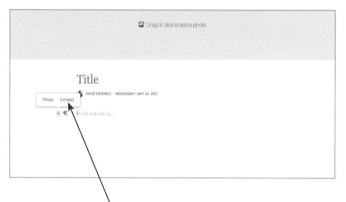

6 You can embed images or videos from the web. Select **Embed**. Copy the media's web address and paste it into the box. Click **Insert**

7 A photo can also be added to the document's header. Click the header, and choose a photo or drag an image to it

8 To let others edit the document, tick the box for **Allow other members to edit this document**

9 When you are finished, click **Publish**

If you link to a file stored on Dropbox, anyone outside the Group could potentially view it.

Uploading a file to Groups

As long as a Group's settings permit it, members are able to upload files. These can be downloaded by other members, again depending on the settings that have been applied to the Group.

1 Go to a Group and click the three-dot **More** button in the Create Post box

2 Select **Add File**

3 Click **Choose File** and find a file, whether that is on your computer or stored in the cloud. The maximum file size is 100MB

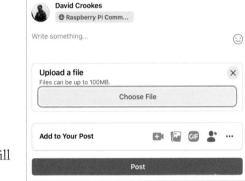

4 The filename will be displayed. If you have chosen the wrong file, you can repeat Step 3 and choose another file

5 Explain what the file is and what you expect others to do with it by typing in the area that says **Write something**

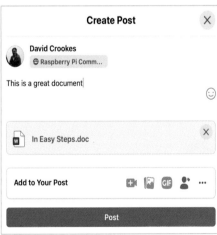

6 When ready, click **Post** and the file will be shared with the Group

Viewing content on a mobile

If you want to keep a close eye on the content being uploaded to a Group, why not do so while you're on the move using the Facebook app?

1 With the Facebook app open, go to the Group you wish to view and select the three-dot **Menu** button

2 You will be presented with a large number of options:

Member Requests. Tap this to see a list of people who want to be a member. They can be approved or declined.

Following. Decide if you want to continue following a Group. If you deselect this, you'll remain a member but won't receive alerts.

Pin Group. Groups you like most can be pinned so that they appear at the top of your Group list.

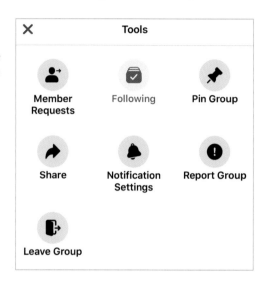

Share. Opt to share a Group to your News Feed, share it in Messenger, or copy the link.

Notification Settings. You can determine how you receive notifications, whether within the app or on your device.

Report Group. Something not quite right? Let Facebook know.

Leaving a Group via mobile
As you can see at the bottom of the Tools menu, there is also an option to leave a Group.

Tapping this prompts you to confirm that you want to leave. You can opt to turn off notifications for new posts instead.

Creating your own Group

Once you've familiarized yourself with how Groups work, you may decide to take the plunge and set up one of your own. You can create a Group about any subject you wish, as long as it isn't anything that could be deemed offensive.

1 Click **Groups** in Facebook's left-hand menu

2 Click the **+ Create New Group** button, which you'll find toward the top of the screen

3 You will now see the **Create New Group** window. Decide on a name, and type it into the box marked **Group name**

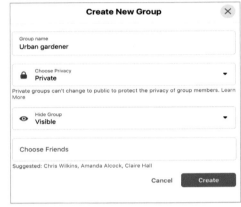

4 Select how private you want your Group to be. A public Group allows anyone access to view content and the list of members. A private Group only allows members to view the posts and who is involved

5 Decide if you want anyone to be able to find your Group by searching for it or whether it should only be discoverable by members

6 Enter the names of the people that you want to invite. Use the suggestions or type names into the Search box

7 Click **Create** when you have finished filling in the fields and your Group will be ready. It won't look much to begin with, but it is now time to start building it up by inviting more people and encouraging them to interact with the Group

Becoming familiar with the Group admin layout

Before we continue on to specific tasks, let's look at the general layout of a Group from the perspective of an administrator (i.e. you). As you will see there are essentially two frames: the Admin Tools run down the left-hand side and the Group's content is located in the main panel to the right.

A shortcut to your Group is created. This will appear in the left-hand menu of Facebook to make it easier to visit your Group in the future.

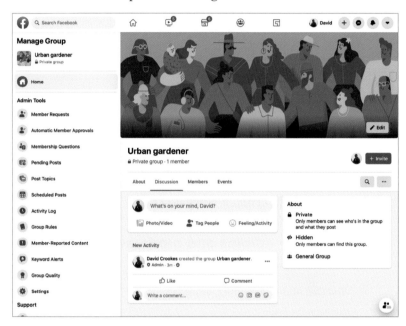

You are able to:

- **Deal with member requests**. It's possible to filter requests by age, gender and even according to when they joined Facebook. You can also view only those members you've invited and those with mutual friends.

- **Set up requirements for automatically approving members**. This can save time by instantly adding those who fit your criteria.

- **Monitor questions**. Pending members can ask up to three questions and you can view and answer them.

- **Create rules**. Start as you mean to go on by writing up to 10 rules that members are expected to abide by.

Approving new members

Even though you can add new members to your Group, you are not alone. Group members can add friends of people in the Group too. We looked at how to send invites earlier in this chapter, but here we explain how you can better control who is allowed into any Groups you create.

1 Click **Group** in the left-hand menu of Facebook and click a Group you want to work with under the **Groups You Manage** section

2 Select **Settings** in the left-hand menu

3 You will see a setting for **Manage Membership**

4 If you want to ultimately approve who can become a member, click the **Edit** button to the right of **Who Can Approve Member Requests**

5 Select **Only admins and moderators**

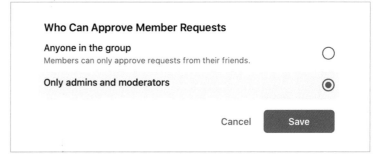

Who Can Approve Member Requests

Anyone in the group
Members can only approve requests from their friends. ○

Only admins and moderators ◉

Cancel   Save

6 Click **Save**

Approving all Group posts
Ensure you approve any posts created by a Group member.

1 Follow Steps 1 and 2 above and look for **Approve All Member Posts**, clicking the **Edit** button to the right

2 Tick the box for **Posts by members must be approved by an admin or a moderator**

Creating extra Group admins

You'll have seen from the previous page that admins and moderators can approve members. Here, we look at how you can create additional admins and moderators to work alongside yourself in looking after your Group.

1 Go to your Group and click **Members** located beneath the main header

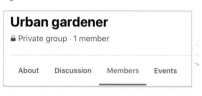

2 You will see a list of the members that are currently in your Group. Click the three-dot **Menu** button to the right of their name

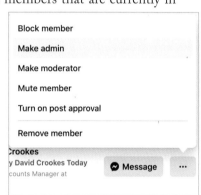

3 Click either **Make admin** or **Make moderator**

4 An invitation will be sent to that person

If you decide you don't want a member to be an admin or moderator, follow Steps 1 and 2, and select Remove as Admin.

What can admins and moderators do?

Once you make someone an admin, they can:

- Make other members admins and moderators.

- Remove admins and moderators.

- Alter the settings for the Group.

Moderators cannot do any of these. Both admins and moderators can, however:

- Approve or refuse posts and membership requests.

- Remove comments, posts and people.

- Pin and unpin posts.

- Look at the support inbox.

Blocking and removing members

Unfortunately, as you build up a Group you may feel the need to remove a member and, to prevent them from returning, go as far as blocking them.

You may want to block somebody because:

● You don't want them to see the Group's posts.

● They are writing abusive posts.

● They are being abusive toward other members of the Group.

● Some other personal or professional reason.

You do not have to tell a person why they are being removed or blocked from your Group.

Removing and blocking a member

1 Go to your Group and select **Members**

2 Click the three-dot **Menu** button to the right of the person whose membership you want to remove

3 Select **Remove member**. If they want to return, they will have to ask for permission

4 You have options to remove their activity from the last seven days or block them. Doing the latter prevents them even finding your Group when they search

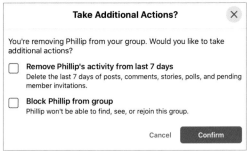

5 Select **Confirm**

6 Blocked people are listed on the Members page under the Blocked tag. You can opt to unblock them if you wish

Adding content via mobile

You can add content to your Group in the way we explained earlier. You can also create content via a mobile device.

1 Go to a Group in the Facebook app on your mobile device and tap the box that says **Write something...**

Mobile devices are great for checking in on Groups when you're on the move.

2 You will see a menu that has options for starting a live video (go to page 148 for more about this). You can also create a Group poll using the same structure explained on page 74, and begin a Watch Party (which we explain more about on page 147). There are options, too, for creating a Group

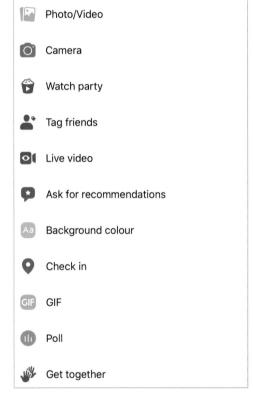

Photo/Video

Camera

Watch party

Tag friends

Live video

Ask for recommendations

Background colour

Check in

GIF

Poll

Get together

event (which we discuss in Chapter 9), asking for recommendations, and sharing GIFs

3 Those of you using iOS will also see an option called **Sell something**. We look more closely at the principles of selling items on Facebook in Chapter 11

4 Tap any of these options to create content for a Group using your mobile device

Personalizing your Group

Until you and your Group's members begin to add content, your Group will feel rather empty. But as well as producing posts, you can flesh your Group out by adding a description. You can also help others to find your Group more easily using tags and even add a location, which is perfect for flagging up the venue of a wedding or your organization's base.

Adding a description

Describing what your Group is about is a good way to encourage anybody stumbling across it to consider requesting to become a member. You can also use it to assure anyone looking specifically for your Group that they have the correct one.

1 Go to your Group and click **Settings**, which you'll find under Admin Tools

2 The top section, Set Up Group, includes an entry called **Name and Description**. Click the **Edit** button to the right of this

> **Set Up Group**
>
> Name and Description

3 As well as being able to change the name, you can write your description within the text box. Ensure it really captures the spirit of what your Group is all about

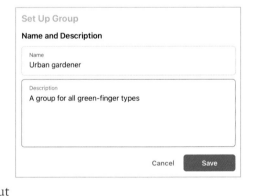

4 Click **Save** when you have finished and the description will be added to your Group

Customizing the Group

You can create an easily remembered web address for your Group, change the color and allow badges to be placed next to members to indicate their status or engagement with the Group.

1 Go to your Group and click **Settings**, which you'll find under Admin Tools

2 Look for the **Customize Group** section and click **Web Address**

3 Complete the web address with a word

www.facebook.com/groups/
urbangardener

or phrase. You'll be told if it has already been used

4 Click **Save**

5 Now, move on to **Group Color** and use the circles to indicate which color should be used for buttons and other elements of your Group page, clicking **Save** when done

6 Finally, decide whether people should receive badges. These can be reserved for administrators, moderators, new members, rising stats, people who share engaging media, and conversation starters. Tick the boxes and **Save**

Adding a location

Where location is important to your Group (for instance, if you want to bring people in your community together for a cake sale), you can use a location tag, making the Group easier to find.

1 Go to your Group, click **Settings** under Admin Tools and click **Location** under Set Up Group

2 Type your location in the Search bar and pick a suggested option, or press **Enter** on your computer's keyboard

3 Click **Save**

Hot tip

You can also indicate the type of Group you are running. It will be set to General by default but click Group Type under Add Extra Features in your Group's settings to change it if you wish.

Uploading a cover image

Nothing personalizes a Group more than a photo. You can use an image to create a striking header for your Group.

To make your cover image stand out:

● Use a clean, bold photo rather than something too busy.

● Consider using art software to create an image that incorporates the name of the Group.

● Ensure it is 1,640 pixels wide and 856 pixels tall to prevent overstretching or blurriness.

● Make it relevant to the theme of your Group.

1 If you have an image on your computer you want to use, then in the banner at the top of your Group, click **Edit**

2 If you want to use a photo that has been posted to your Group, select **Choose from group photos**

3 If you have previously uploaded an image to Facebook and you'd like to use that, click **Choose from my photos**

    Choose from group photos
    Choose from my photos
    Choose from illustrations
    Upload photo

4 Alternatively, select **Choose from illustrations** to choose from a small number of built-in alternatives

5 Or, simply click **Upload photo** and select an image from your computer

Creating an announcement

Some posts can be more significant than others. Perhaps you have written some rules that you want Group members to follow, or maybe you are looking to flag up some important information and ensure that everyone who visits the Group will see it.

You can easily stress the importance of a post.

1 Identify the Group post you want to pin to the top, and click the three-dot **Menu** button in the right-hand corner

2 Select **Mark as announcement** from the menu. This will place it at the top of the Group in an announcements section. Any other posts that the Group members make will be positioned underneath

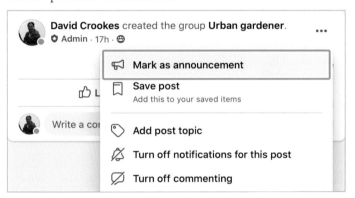

3 If you wish to remove the pin, click the three-dot **Menu** button again, and select **Remove announcement**

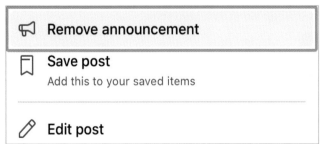

4 Members can Like and Comment on announcements

Deleting a Group

Has your Group come to its natural end? Have you decided that you don't want to continue with it anymore? Or, has it simply not proved to be as popular as you hoped? You don't actually need a reason to close and delete your Group.

1 Before you are able to close a Group, you have to formally remove each member of it. So, go to your Group and click **Members**

2 Go down the entire list of people, clicking the three-dot **Menu** button next to their name and selecting **Remove member** for each one

3 Once you have removed everybody from the Group, you will be left with just yourself. Again, click the three-dot **Menu** button, but this time select **Leave group**

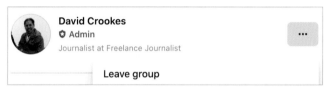

4 With that action, the Group will be deleted

Keeping your options open by archiving the Group

Perhaps deleting a Group feels too drastic a move. As the admin for a Group, you can archive it instead. This allows members to continue visiting, but nobody will be able to post to it or add other people. Archived Groups can be brought back to life by unarchiving them at a later date.

1 On your Group page, click the three-dot **Menu** button

2 Select **Archive Group**

3 When you visit the Group in the future, you'll see a message saying it has been archived, and a prominent option marked **Unarchive Group**

7 Using Portal

Facebook Portal is a smart device that makes it easier to connect with family and friends. Focused around a camera, Portal is ideal for engaging in video chats and there's a special feature that will bring story telling for children to life. It also doubles as a digital picture frame, so memories can be just a glance away.

What is Facebook Portal?

Facebook Portal is a set of video communication devices that make it easier for you to keep in contact with your family and friends. Making use of Artificial Intelligence (AI) technology, it is designed to make you feel as if you are in the same room as the people you are talking to.

All Portals come with Amazon's voice assistant Alexa built in.

This is achieved by allowing the camera to follow your movements in a room. If you walk out of shot, it will pan and zoom to bring you back in. Portal will also minimize background noise, ensuring that everyone can hear each other more clearly.

Since it's always hands-free, this means you can concentrate entirely on your conversation. In fact, you can even initiate a chat by saying, "Hey Portal".

There are, however, different versions of Facebook Portal and which one you decide to choose depends on how much you are willing to spend, the size of the screen and the experience that you are after.

You can buy:

- **Portal Mini**. This is the cheapest device and it comes with an 8-inch high-definition display. It offers a 114-degree field of view from a 13MP camera.

- **Portal**. For those wanting a 10-inch HD display. It too has a 114-degree field of view from a 13MP camera.

- **Portal+**. Comes with a 15.6-inch HD display that rotates, allowing the 12.5MP camera to take in a 140-degree field of view. It also has better speakers.

- **Portal TV**. A 12.5MP camera that connects to and fits on top of your television, offering a 120-degree field of view. Unlike the other touchscreen models, this Portal is controlled using a remote device.

Setting up Facebook Portal

So, you've got your shiny new Facebook Portal and you're ready to get going with it. Time to plug it in.

Getting started with Portal Mini, Portal and Portal+

1 When you power up your Portal for the first time, you'll be asked to **Select your language**. The display is touchscreen, so use your finger to scroll the list of languages and tap to select the one you want (note there are four varieties of English). Then, tap **Next**

2 Portal will try to connect to your Wi-Fi. A list of connections will show on the screen so select the one you use, enter its password using the on-screen keyboard and tap **Join**. Then, tap **Next**

3 Tap **Continue** and Portal will download and install the latest software. It can take up to 15 minutes

4 You can now get on with setting up your Portal. Tap **Next** and agree to the terms of service by selecting **Continue** and give your Portal a name. This can be a custom name such as David's Portal or where it will be located. Portal suggests Living room, Kitchen, Dining room, Office and Bedroom. Tap **Next** when done

5 You can connect a WhatsApp account as well as Facebook. But since our focus is on Facebook, tap the box next to **Facebook** and tap **Next**

6 You'll be shown a code. Enter this at **facebook.com/device** using a smartphone or computer. Tap **Continue**, then **Confirm**, and the Portal screen shows Facebook has connected

7 Tap **Next**

Facebook Portal can be used in both the horizontal and vertical position so play around to see what works best for you.

Setting up Portal TV is just as simple. After mounting the device to the top of your TV and removing the plastic battery tab on the remote, press **Select**. The setup will be similar to the other Portal devices. You'll select a language, connect to Wi-Fi, give your Portal a name and you will connect your Facebook account.

Customizing your Portal

After connecting your Portal device to Wi-Fi and your Facebook account, you can begin to tailor it to your needs.

Hot tip

The Portal TV's camera and microphone on/off button is on the side of the device. The Portal TV also has a camera cover to block the lens.

Beware

For security, you may find peace of mind by disabling the camera and microphone when you don't need them. Just use the physical switch on the Portal device.

1 Set your favorite contacts by going down the list of people who you are likely to connect with most often, and tapping the box next to their name

2 Their profile images will appear at the bottom of the screen. Tap **Add** when you have finished

3 You can also decide whether or not to hide some contacts. Doing so means you will not be able to connect with them using your Portal device. If you wish to do this, tap **Hide Some Contacts** and select the names of those you wish to hide before tapping **Hide**. If you do not wish to do this, tap **Continue With All Contacts**

4 Now, test your camera. Tap **Try It** and ensure that the camera is turned on. You do this by sliding the switch that is on the frame. As you walk around the room you will notice that the camera follows you, zooming and panning to ensure your face is in the picture. Of course, if you wander too far away, you'll be out of shot but this is a good way to experiment with Portal's limits. Tap **Next**

5 The setup process also lets you connect third-party accounts such as Spotify. Look down the list for suggestions and tap **Connect** next to any you want to connect. You'll be taken to another screen that prompts you to confirm the connection and you'll be asked to enter the account's login details. In the case of Spotify, this would give you access to music, so long as you have an account with the service. Tap **Next**

6 Want to add photos from your phone's Camera Roll? If not, tap **Not Now**; otherwise, install the Portal app on your smartphone. We cover this on page 103

7 Now, set up Alexa. This requires you to connect your Amazon account and we cover this on page 99. If you don't want to do this or if you do not have an Amazon account, then tap **Not now** and tap **Continue** when you are asked to confirm that you'll consider this later

8 It's time to set up Portal's own voice-recognition personal digital assistant. It means you can say, "Hey Portal" to initiate, answer or end calls but you will need to decide if you want your voice commands to be stored by Facebook. Doing so lets Facebook retain recordings and transcriptions and these can be reviewed by people hired by Facebook. Such work assists in improving the feature but bear in mind background conversations can be picked up. View interactions by going to the Facebook website, clicking the downward arrow in the top-right corner and selecting **Settings & Privacy** > **Activity log**

9 Tap **Explore Home** and you're ready to use your Portal device. You can embark on a quick guided tour of the features and we'd recommend you become familiar with the interface by going through this

Starting a chat with Portal

So long as your Facebook friends have a Facebook account or you have contacts on WhatsApp, you can make a call to them from your Portal device.

It doesn't matter if the person you're calling doesn't have a Portal device of their own because the calls will connect via the Messenger app and website, the Facebook website and the WhatsApp app.

Using your voice to initiate a call

1 Say "**Hey Portal, call**" and speak the name of the person you want to connect with

2 Their name will be read and you'll be asked to confirm it is correct. If so, say "**Yes**" and the call will be made

3 You can also say "**Hey Portal, cancel**" or "**Hey Portal, hang up**"

Using the Portal screen (not applicable for Portal TV)

1 You have three main methods. Either:

- Tap **Call People** on the first Home screen.
- Swipe left and tap the **Contacts app**.
- Tap a contact listed under your **Favorites**.

2 Selecting their name gives you options to video chat, make an audio call, send a message or add the contact to your Favorites if you have not already. Tap the relevant icon to make your choice. (For the first two options in Step 1, you will also see a video icon that can be used to initiate a video chat)

3 The Portal will start your call

4 You can end a call by tapping the red button

To accept an incoming call on your Portal, tap **Answer** (or use the Play button on the remote of Portal TV) and you will be instantly connected. You can also say, "**Hey Portal, answer**".

Using Portal TV? Go to the **Contacts** app and select the person to call using the remote.

Making a Group call on Portal

Conversations can be held with more than one other person so why not call multiple members of your family or get together with a few friends?

1 Start a conversation with a single person, following the steps on page 94

2 While you are on the call, tap the screen to show the menu. Then, tap the **Add Person** icon (the option displayed to the far left)

3 Select the person you wish to add

4 When they accept the call, they will be added to your chat, allowing them to join in the conversation

Finding people to call

1 Go to the **Contacts** app on the second Home screen on your Portal device

2 You will see five headings:

- **Suggested**: Favorite contacts and others you call regularly.

- **Recents**: People taken from your call history.

- **Messenger**: Contacts drawn from Facebook.

- **WhatsApp**: Contacts drawn from WhatsApp.

- **Rooms**: This allows you to make use of Messenger Rooms, essentially creating a group of people to interact with (see page 96).

3 Choose a category or tap the **Search** icon in the top left-hand corner to manually look for a contact to call

Chatting in a Messenger Room

A good way to chat with a group of people is to invite them to join you in a Room. You can also join Rooms that have been set up by other people. Discover more about Messenger Rooms on pages 120 to 122.

Hot tip

You can have as many as 50 people in a Messenger Room.

Creating a Room

1 Go to the **Contacts** app and select **Rooms** (you may have to swipe left on the options at the top of the screen)

2 Select **Create room**

3 Select **Room activity** and indicate the nature of your planned conversation

4 Select **Who can discover and join?** and decide if you only want to invite friends or whether you wish to open it up to anyone with the link you'll be provided with

5 Select **Next** and either allow all your Facebook friends to discover and join the Room or restrict it to specific invitees

6 Select the box next to those you're inviting and tap **Done**

7 Select **Start Room** and select **Join Room** when ready

Joining a Room

1 Open the **Contacts app** and select **Rooms**. If you see a Room you'd like to join, select it

2 If you have been sent a Room link, tap **Join room with a link** and input it using the on-screen keyboard

Looking your best on screen

One of the perils of video calls is the worry that you're not looking presentable enough. Don't bother with a mirror. Portal devices have a way of letting you check how you look.

1 Select the name of the person you want to call in the **Contacts** app

2 Beneath the options to start a call, you'll see **Check Self-view**. Select to see yourself on the screen

3 Like what you see? Tap **Start Call** or else tap **Not Now**

Blurring the background

1 Follow Steps 1 to 2 above

2 Select the raindrop icon and the background will blur

3 For a fun background, select the magic wand icon instead and choose **Backgrounds**. Swipe through the large selection: there's a beach, an airplane and the moon

Playing around with the effects

1 Play around with fun effects too. Instead of choosing Backgrounds select **Featured**, selecting the cartoon circles to change yourself into different characters

2 **Music videos** puts you in the midst of a funky tune while **Cool** lets you choose from headphones, caps and more. Present yourself inside **Cards**, enjoy some **Family Fun** and be as **Ridiculous** as you want

3 Tap **Start Call** when you've found a great look

Ensuring you can see and hear

Is the volume too low or could you benefit from increasing the brightness of the screen? Portal devices have a set of controls that let you work out the most suitable settings.

Using a Portal device

1 Swipe up in the Portal screen to reveal the control panel

2 Use your finger to swipe left and right on the volume slider. Move it right to increase the volume

3 Do the same for the brightness control

4 You can also activate **Do Not Disturb**, which ensures your Portal device won't allow incoming calls until 8am the following morning

Using a Portal TV

1 Go to **Settings** from the Home screen

2 Select **General**

3 Select **Audio** and **Portal volume**

4 Turn up the volume using the right navigation button on your remote and turn it down using the left button

5 Adjust the brightness control on your television itself if the image is too dim or bright. Refer to your TV manual for more details on how to do this

Hot tip

The alarm volume can be adjusted in the Portal's Settings app.

Hot tip

Tap **Display** in the Settings app and determine whether you only want to show the clock in low lighting. You can also opt to tint the screen amber to reduce eye strain and activate or deactivate automatic screen brightness.

Setting up Alexa on Portal

Alexa is one of the world's most popular personal digital assistants. You can ask it for a weather forecast, set a reminder, ask for suggestions and even get it to tell you a joke. Indeed, Alexa can perform many tasks and the feature is available on your Portal device.

1 Go to the **Settings** app on your Portal

2 Tap **Accounts**

3 Select **Amazon Alexa**

4 Go to **amazon.com/code** in a web browser and select your account if you're already logged in (otherwise sign in using your username and password)

5 Enter the code displayed on your Portal device into the box on the website

6 Click **Continue** on your Portal. Doing so means you agree with Amazon's Conditions of Use and Sale

The settings for setting up Alexa on Portal TV follow the same set of instructions shown here.

amazon

Register Your Device

Enter the code that you found on your device so we can register it with your Amazon account. Then click on "Continue" to proceed to the next step.

e.g. XB5GQ

Continue

7 Alexa is now ready and you can tap **Done**

Adjusting Alexa's settings

1 Follow Steps 1 to 3 above

2 Tap **Sounds** to have sound playing at the start and end of your requests to Alexa. This is a good way to confirm when Alexa is listening

3 Tap **Restrict Access** if you want to block searches for film trailers

Some apps are available when you are in the midst of a call. Tap the Entertainment icon and you can choose from Story Time (page 101), Watch (page 102), AR games, photo casting, effects and Spotify.

Portal TV also lets you access the video-streaming apps, Netflix and Prime Video. If you bought your Portal TV after October 6, 2020, you may find there are buttons for these services on the remote control. Just log in using a Netflix or Prime Video account to access the services.

Exploring the device's apps

Portal has many built-in apps as well as a store where you can download and install many more. These include:

- **Spotify**: The music-streaming app that allows you to choose from millions of songs.

- **Photobooth**: This lets you create fun cards as well as images and videos that you can share in Messenger. The options are similar to those discussed on page 97 under Play around with the effects.

- **Gaming**: A selection of games including Dominoes: Battle!, Chess, Ludo Club, Battleship and Words With Friends. These can be played with friends by tapping the relevant option after launching each title and choosing people to play against.

- **Browser**: Surf the web by typing in a web address or selecting one of a number of suggested websites such as YouTube, Wikipedia and Allrecipes.

Launching an app

1 Swipe left from the first Portal Home screen to see a selection of apps

2 Tap the one you wish to use

Finding more apps

1 Tap the icon for **Apps**

2 Select the **Apps** tab and go down the list, looking for apps that you may like

3 Tap **Add** to download it

4 You will find shortcuts to websites under the **Websites** tab

5 Again, go down the list and select **Add**

Telling an engaging story

You don't have to be sitting comfortably in the same room as your grandchildren to tell them a fun story. You can use the Story Time app on Portal and turn yourself into many colorful characters as you bring an assortment of tales to life.

1 Ensure your Portal is in landscape mode

2 Tap **Contacts** and choose who you need to video call

3 During the call, tap the **Entertainment** icon

4 Tap **Story Time** and choose a tale. Look through new releases, check out a range of featured tales, including Little Red Riding Hood and Goldie and the Three Bears, or pick characters such as Pete the Cat and Otto the Dog

5 Discover how long the story will last and read a synopsis by selecting **Description**

6 When you're ready and the children are settled, tap **Play**

7 The story will play. Swipe left and begin to read the story. Music will accompany your story and clever technology will place animation and Augmented Reality (AR) effects on the screen, making you integral to the story

Are you in the same room? Then launch the Story Time app and you and a child can read along with any of the stories together.

For those using Portal TV, click Select when you're in the midst of a call. Choose **Story Time**.

Can't see Facebook Watch on Portal TV? Visit the Portal's app store and install it.

Hot tip

It is also possible to livestream from a Portal device to your Facebook profile. Launch the app on Portal (and confirm your login to go live by following the on-screen instructions) and allow the device's Smart Camera to keep you in the frame as you make your broadcast.

Watching videos on Portal

When you're not catching up with family and friends, the Portal screen is perfect for watching videos. View these alone or even in sync with others thanks to the inclusion of Facebook Watch.

1 Visit your Portal device's Home screen and select **Watch**

2 Look down the left-hand menu for **Channels**, **Live videos** and **News**, and choose a category

3 You will also see the **Your Videos** category. This will be filled with any videos you save as well as your viewing history and highlights from pages you follow. You will need to sync your Facebook account to view these by going to **facebook.com/device** and entering the code displayed on the Portal screen

4 Tap or select any video thumbnail to watch. You're able to Like videos, save them by tapping the bookmark icon or share them to your Timeline. You can ensure you see future videos from a creator by selecting **Follow** and there is an option to **View Page**, where you will find other videos the creator may have made

5 If you select the three-dot **Menu** button when you watch a video, you can hide it, snooze the creator for 30 days, hide all videos from the creator or report it

Watching videos with other people

1 Start a video chat (see page 94) and, while you are talking, select the **Entertainment** icon

2 Select **Watch**

3 A series of videos will be made available for you to view. Select one and wait for the other person to **Accept**, allowing you to enjoy the video together

Using Portal to frame photos

Your Portal can be used as a digital photo frame, allowing you to display images when the device is in standby mode. You can select which images you want using the Photos app on Portal or via the Portal app on a mobile phone.

Tap **Your Portal** in the Portal app and you can use it to call your device, access your favorite contacts and update them or select photos that you'd like to appear on a nearby Portal without adding them to your device.

Using the Photos app on Portal

1 Tap the Photos app on your Portal and confirm your login by visiting **facebook.com/device** in a browser and entering the code displayed on the Portal (you could use your Facebook password or opt to set up a passcode to avoid visiting the website for this step in the future)

2 View any images uploaded to Facebook (you can link an Instagram account if you have one, for more images)

3 Tap an image and use the switch to display it on your Portal

Using the Portal app on a mobile device

1 Download the Portal app from the App Store for iOS and Google Play Store for Android

2 View any images you have uploaded to Facebook and tap any you like. Or, tap **Portal photos** and create a new album for Portal using images from your phone

3 Tap **Add Photos** and browse your images, tapping those you want to use. When you're ready, tap **Add**

4 To ensure images are shown on your Portal, tap **Display on Portal** when it is shown as an option

Creating notes on Portal

It's easy to forget things but, with Portal, you can ensure you're reminded of the important stuff. It comes with a built-in Notes app that lets you leave written and drawn notes or even record audio and video. These are displayed when the device is in standby mode.

1 Tap the **Notes** app icon to launch it. You'll find this in the list of apps and also on the standby screen

2 Choose the sort of note you want to create:

- **Text**: This lets you use the on-screen keyboard to make a written note. Use the **Aa** icon to change the font and alter the background color if you wish.

- **Drawing**: Use your finger to draw on the screen. Again, you can change the background color and there's also an Erase function if you make a mistake.

- **Photo** or **Video**: Access the Portal camera and tap the main circular button to take a photograph or make a recording. You will have access to effects and a countdown timer.

3 Tap the circular blue tick when you've finished creating a text or drawing-based note or tap **Save to Notes** after taking a photo or recording a video

4 The notes will begin to appear on the Portal device when it is in standby mode

5 Tap a note to view it

6 Tapping the note again will enlarge it and show a Trash can icon with an option to delete. You can also delete a note by pressing and holding down on it when you are on the standby screen, again tapping the Trash can

You can only display three notes on the standby screen at any one time so bear that in mind if you want a constant reminder of something particularly important. Tapping a note will show you any other notes that you have created.

Don't want to see the notes on the standby screen at all? Tap the **X** on the icon and you can remove it. Want it back? Tap Settings, select Display and use the slider next to Notes to reactivate it.

8 Using Facebook Messenger

There will be moments when you just want to have a private conversation with a friend or a group of people. This chapter shows how you can use Messenger to send text, video or photo messages; play games; and even make voice and video calls to your friends for free.

What is Messenger?

Although you may be used to texting your friends, family members, colleagues and others, there are many alternatives to the standard text messaging services built into today's phones.

Referred to as instant messaging apps, they have become hugely popular. Services such as WhatsApp and Google Hangouts typically allow you to use the internet to send messages, images and documents, and make voice and video calls.

Yet one service – Facebook Messenger – has been growing at a blistering rate. Indeed, with more than 1.2 billion users, it is now one of the world's largest instant messaging apps and a social network in its own right.

It is not bad-going for a service that only began in 2014, when Facebook made the decision to split the ability to message people using the Facebook app into a separate Messenger application. Available for Android and iOS, as well as on your computer desktop via an app or in an internet browser, it lets you:

- **Text chat without needing a cell phone number**. You only need to be connected with the person you wish to contact.

- **Make voice and video calls**. Face-to-face conversations are easy, and you are even able to send voice recordings.

- **Set up group chats**. If you want to share information or have a conversation with more than one person, you can.

- **Take and send photos and videos**. Sharing media is simple, and you can snap images and record videos from within the Messenger app.

- **Have lots of fun**. You can use stickers and GIFs. Children and grandchildren love these and they won't fail to bring a smile to your face.

What's more, you can get set up without needing to create a new account. Simply use your Facebook username and password.

Installing Messenger

Since Messenger is a separate app, you will need to install it alongside Facebook on your phone or tablet.

Installing on Android

1 Tap the Play Store icon on your Android Home screen

2 Search for **Messenger** using the Search bar at the top of the screen

3 Select the entry that bears the logo

4 Tap **Install**

Hot tip

You can also access Messenger on the web at **messenger.com** or by selecting the Messenger icon in Facebook. Visit **messenger.com/desktop** if you'd like the desktop app for Windows 10 or macOS. This gives you the same features as on the mobile app and it's particularly good when using Messenger Rooms.

Installing on iOS

1 Tap the App Store icon on your iOS Home screen

2 Tap the Search icon at the bottom of the screen, and type **Messenger** in the Search bar that appears

3 Look for Messenger in the search results list, and tap **Get** when you see it

4 Tap **Install**

Hot tip

Is the white glare of Messenger too much for your eyes? Then tap your profile picture in Messenger to visit the settings and tap **Dark Mode** for the option to turn it on or off.

Setting up Messenger

There are two ways of opening Messenger on your smartphone or tablet device:

- **Tap the app icon**. You will find this on the Home screen of your device.

- **Tap the Messenger icon in Facebook**. You will find this in the top right-hand corner of the Facebook app.

From there, you will be taken through some initial steps aimed at setting up the Messenger app.

Getting started

1 Select whether or not you already have a Facebook account. We're assuming that you do since you have got this far into the book, so tap **I have a Facebook account**. It is worth bearing in mind that if

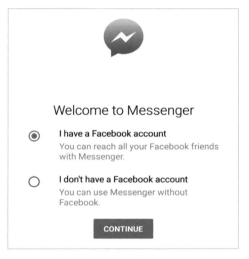

you ever decide not to use Facebook in the future, you can still use Messenger without it

2 Enter the email or phone number that you used when signing up to Facebook, and type in your password in order to log in

Allowing others to reach you

To make the most of Messenger, you may want to widen the number of people you can contact through it. Messenger will continue to take you through this setup process.

1 You should see a screen entitled **Text anyone in your phone**. This is Messenger's way of asking to access your contacts and it will use the information it finds to see how many of your friends, colleagues, relatives and others are also using Messenger

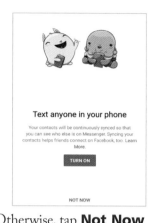

You don't have to be a Facebook user to use Messenger. This also means you can contact non-Facebook users using Messenger.

2 Decide whether or not you want Messenger to do this. If you do, simply tap the **Turn On** button. Otherwise, tap **Not Now**

3 If you do decline the offer and change your mind, don't worry: you can do it later. Tap your profile image at the top of the Messenger screen, select **People** and turn on **Sync Contacts**

Adding your phone number

If you do not have a phone number associated with your Facebook account, Messenger will ask you to input it (tap **Not Now** if you do not want to do this).

1 Tap the country shown on the screen and change it to the territory your number is associated with

2 Enter your phone number

3 Tap **OK**

4 If you decline to do this right now, you can do it later. Tap your profile image at the top of the Messenger screen, select **Phone** and enter it from there

Understanding the interface

Facebook Messenger packs a lot of information and many sections onto its main screen. But take a small amount of time to familiarize yourself, and you'll soon feel comfortable with it.

Familiarizing yourself with Messenger's layout

We look at the Messenger screen in Android here and, as you can see, it is split into a small number of sections. The available options make it easy for you to communicate with other users.

Camera. Take a photo or record a video.

Your profile. Tapping this icon gives you access to your Messenger profile, account settings and preferences.

Search. Look for people and Groups by tapping the Search bar and typing a search term.

Write a message. When you are ready to type and send a message, select this icon.

People. Search for people, add contacts, check who is active and view which of your contacts are also using Facebook Messenger.

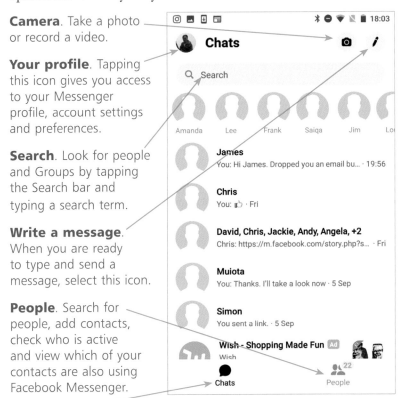

Chats. This tab displays a list of messages you have sent and received, as you can see in this screenshot.

You will see from the messages that have been received here that you are given the name of the contact, the time or day when the message was received and a preview of the message.

Adverts also appear within the chat list. These are clearly marked.

...cont'd

Messenger's layout in iOS

As with the Android screenshot of Messenger, we have deliberately obscured the profile images.

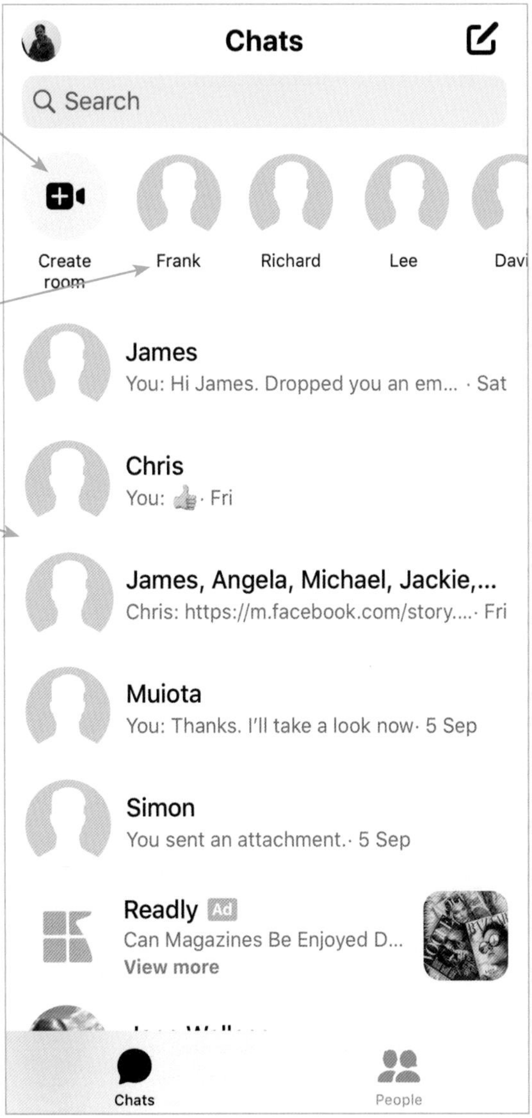

Create room. If you want to set up a video chat, then you can create a room. This will allow you to invite others using a link.

Active contacts. If your contacts are currently using Messenger, then they will appear here.

Chats. Your recent conversations appear here. The latest messages appear at the top, and you can also see when they were sent.

More conversations. Keep scrolling to see more of your chats. If you have lots of chats, they will keep loading onto the screen until you reach the end. You are also allowed to have

as many chat threads as you like, so don't worry about connecting with others and enjoying your many conversations.

111

Writing and sending a message

One of the first things you will want to do when you start using Messenger is write and send somebody a message. There are two key ways of doing this:

- Start a new conversation with somebody.

- Respond to an established thread.

Starting a new conversation

1 Tap the **Chats** tab and select the **Write Message** icon located in the top-right corner

2 Choose the person you wish to chat with. You can add multiple names if you wish to hold a conversation with more than one person

Responding to an established thread

1 Tap the **Chats** tab

2 Scroll down the list of conversations, and tap the message you want to respond to

Creating the message

After establishing who you want to send your message to, you are now ready to create it.

1 Look toward the bottom of the screen. You will see a box containing the letters Aa. Tap this **Text box** to bring the keyboard onto the screen

2 Start typing your message using the keyboard

3 When you have finished, tap the **Send** button

You can send and request money through Messenger if you live in the US (*correct at the time of printing*). To send money, start a conversation with a friend, tap the **+** sign, then tap **$**. The first time you use the service, Messenger will ask you to set up a payment account. Once done, just enter the amount, tap **Pay**, and add a debit card. To receive money, open a conversation and tap **Accept Money**.

Sending stickers and GIFs

They say a picture paints a thousand words, and that is also true when you're creating messages in Messenger. You can send:

- **Stickers**. Fun illustrated pictures and animations.

- **GIFs**. Hilarious moving images with no sound.

- **Emojis**. Digital images used to express ideas and emotions.

1 Tap the smiley face in the **Text box**

2 Select either the **Stickers** or the **GIF** tab

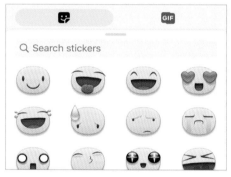

3 After selecting **Stickers**, you can look through the images. Tap one you would like to use, and it will appear in the Text box

4 To prevent endless scrolling, Messenger allows you to search for stickers using the **Search Stickers** Text box

5 If you select **GIFs**, you will see a set of moving images. Try typing various search terms if you wish to look for something more specific. GIFs cover a large range of subject matters

Want even more choice? When selecting Stickers, tap the **Store** icon located to the far right of the toolbar running along the bottom of the screen. It looks like a market stall in iOS and a downward arrow in Android. This gives you access to the Sticker Store for extra goodies.

For emojis, either select the Emoji tab in Android or tap the smiley face located in the bottom-left corner of the keyboard in iOS.

113

Sending a photo or video

You can attach photos and videos to your messages. They can be:

- Photos or videos stored on your device.

- Photos or videos taken fresh using the camera from within the Messenger app.

Sending a previously-saved photograph or video

1 There are a set of icons to the left of the Text box (if you cannot see them all in iOS, tap the arrow icon)

2 Tap the **Photo** icon

3 A selection of images will appear at the bottom of the screen. Allow Messenger to access your photos and scroll through them. Tap the one you want to send to your contact

4 You will have a choice to **Edit** or **Send** the image

5 We will look at editing images in greater depth in Chapter 10 but, for now, tapping **Send** will create a message using your photo and send it on its way

6 The image will appear in the conversation thread

7 You will also see a **Share** button next to the image in the conversation thread. Tap this if you wish to send the image to another friend or to a Group

...cont'd

Sending a new photograph taken using the camera

1 To take a new photograph, press the **Camera** icon to the left of the Text box

2 Messenger will access your camera so line up your shot and use the shutter button to take it

3 If you are pleased with the image, tap **Send**. You can also opt to **Save** it

Sending a new video recorded using the camera

1 If you want to send a video clip, tap the **Camera** icon

2 In Android, select the option for **Video** beneath the shutter button. In iOS, you can hold down the shutter button. In either case you can record a short video

3 If you are pleased with the video, tap **Send**. You can also opt to **Save** it

Sending a voice message

Whether your fingers are tired or you feel something is just better explained verbally, Messenger will allow you to record and send a voice message.

1 Tap the **Microphone** icon to the left of Messenger's Text box in iOS or tap and hold it in Android

2 Speak and your device's microphone will pick up and record what you are saying

3 If you decide to abandon the message, just drag it up the screen to cancel in Android or tap the Trash can

4 Otherwise, when you let go, the recording will end

5 It will be instantly placed into a message and sent

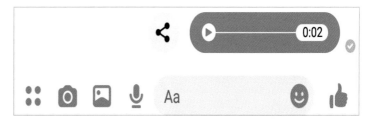

Listening to a recorded voice message

1 When the message is received (and the same applies when you are sent such a message too), you can listen back by tapping the **Play** button within the voice message box that appears in the conversation thread

2 You can tap again to pause it at any point

Forwarding or unsending a message

If you write or receive a message that you would like to send to someone else, you can forward it on. It's also possible to unsend a message, removing it from a thread.

Forwarding your messages

1 Identify a message you want to forward or copy and either press your finger down on it in the mobile app or hover over it on the website

2 If you're using the app, **Forward** appears toward the bottom of the screen. On the website, it's within the three-dot **More** icon that appears next to the message

3 Go down the list of friends or use the search field to manually look for a person. Select

Send next to their name and the message will be sent

Unsending your messages

1 Identify a message you want to unsend. Press your finger down on it in the mobile app or hover over it if you're using the website version

2 Tap **More** in the iOS app or click the three-dot **More** button on the website (if you're using Android, skip this step and go to Step 3)

3 Select **Remove**

4 Tap **Unsend** and the message won't be viewable by those it was originally sent to

5 You can also choose **Remove For You** or **Remove For Everyone**

Beware

Facebook has a forwarding limit that prevents you sending the same message to more than five people or Groups at a time. This is to help slow the spread of fake news.

Hot tip

The **Remove for Everyone** option will appear if you're trying to remove a message within 10 minutes of sending it. A note will be placed in the thread, stating that the message has been removed. If you select **Remove for You**, the message will only disappear from your view but it will remain for others in the thread.

Hot tip

If you receive a map, tap the pin and you'll be able to open it in a map app and get directions.

Sharing your location

While there are some concerns about sharing your location with a wide number of people on Facebook, allowing specific contacts to know your whereabouts can be useful, especially if you are arranging to meet or if you need to help someone find your current location.

1 Tap a conversation thread, or tap the **Write Message** icon and choose a contact

2 Tap the **+** icon to the left of the Text box

3 Select the **Location** icon

4 You must allow Messenger to access the location of your device (for Android, select **Allow** and for iOS go to the **Settings** app and navigate to **Privacy > Location Services**. Scroll down and tap Messenger, then select either **While Using the App** or **Always**)

5 A map will appear on the screen, pinpointing your current location. You can also search for other locations

6 When you have found a location, tap **Start Sharing Live Location** in iOS or tap **Share Live Location** in Android

7 The location will be sent. This will stay live for 60 minutes

Having a secret conversation

By default, your conversations are not fully encrypted. That means they could be potentially intercepted and read, even though the chances of someone doing that are small. If this worries you, there is a way of holding a conversation using end-to-end encryption. By activating it, no-one will be able to read your messages, and that includes Facebook itself.

Using iOS

1 Tap the **Write Message** icon

2 Tap **Secret** in the top right-hand corner

3 Select who you wish to message

4 Now, start writing your message in the usual way

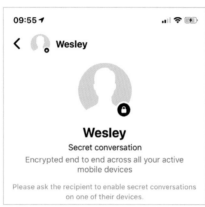

Using Android

1 Choose somebody to start a conversation with

2 Tap the **Info** icon in the top-right corner

3 Tap **Go to Secret Conversation**

4 Start writing your message. Messenger will clearly state that the conversation is being held in secret

Nothing would stop the recipient of your messages (or, indeed, yourself) from taking a screenshot of your secret conversation and sharing that with others.

Messenger will make you aware that new secret conversations will only be available on the device you are using. That means the conversation won't appear in Messenger apps on other platforms.

Use the Timer button in the Text box to set how long your message should appear for.

Chatting in Messenger Rooms

Being able to chat face to face over video is a wonderful way to keep in touch with friends and family, particularly if you're unable to meet in person on a regular basis. With Messenger Rooms, you can initiate a video chat and invite others to join you. What's more, those you want to chat to won't even need a Facebook account of their own.

Hot tip

A Room can also be started within Facebook itself. In the Create Post box, you will see an option titled **Room**. Tapping this gives you options to select an activity, invite people and indicate a start time.

Hot tip

Messenger Rooms can also be accessed using the Messenger desktop app, which can be downloaded from messenger.com/desktop Click the **Create Room** icon shown in Step 1 and a link will be generated. This can be copied then pasted into an email, text or messaging app. Click **Edit** and you can determine whether people with the link or only people on Facebook can join. People can chat with you by clicking the link you provide.

1 In the Chats tab of Messenger, tap the **Create Room** icon located in the top left-hand corner

2 Tap **Room activity** and decide on the focus of your chat. You will see that you can choose from a variety of icons including Coffee chat, TV time, Dinner, and more

3 Tap **Who can join automatically?**. Here, you are going to decide whether you wish to restrict your Room to only those friends and family you invite or whether you want to widen it to anyone who ends up being able to access the link that you'll end up creating

4 Decide if you want to chat now or if you'd prefer to tap **Schedule for later**, in which case you're able to set a date and time. This would work particularly well if you're looking to invite more than a handful of people, ensuring they have enough notice and can make the chat

5 Tap **Create Room** and begin inviting people. You'll see a list of friends and Groups you may want to consider. Tap **Send** next to any you want to invite and they'll be sent an invitation

David's room
Join my room to video chat
David Crookes · Starts now

6 Tap **Join Room** and wait for friends to enter

...cont'd

Receiving an invite

1 A notification is sent to anyone invited to join a Room (and this applies if someone invites you to a Room)

2 By tapping the notification, there will be a button to **Join Room**

3 When someone joins a Room, other people with the link or invitation can see that person

Holding a video chat in Rooms

There are some key icons on the call screen that you should become familiar with. Note that their position may be different on your device.

1 When a chat is in progress you'll see who is involved

2 Use the Camera icon to switch between the front- and back-facing camera on devices

3 Tap the microphone button to mute

4 Take a shot of the screen by tapping the shutter button

5 End the call by tapping on the red phone button

Beware

If you are not connected to Wi-Fi, you may be charged for any data you use when making calls.

Hot tip

You can also directly chat with someone in Messenger without using Rooms. Tap the **People** tab in Messenger, select a person and use the video or phone icons to indicate whether you want to engage in a video or audio call.

121

Don't forget

You can invite up to 50 people to join you in a Messenger Room.

Accessing more Rooms features

When you are engaged in a Rooms chat, swipe up and you will see even more options.

1 Swipe up to view this screen

2 Tapping the link icon will allow you to share an invite link with other people

3 Selecting **Lock room** ensures that no-one is able to enter the Room

4 You can end a room by accessing **Security and Settings**

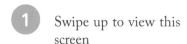

122

Sharing your screen

Being able to share your device's screen with friends and family has many benefits. Someone could show you how to solve a problem with your device by taking you through the issue step by step (or you could assist them). Sharing also means you could browse a selection of photos or even shop together online.

1 Go to **Security and Settings** and you can activate **Screen sharing**

2 You'll see an option for **Share Your Screen** under **Things To Do Together**

3 Tap this and select **Start Sharing**

4 Your camera will be turned off and the content of your screen will be displayed instead. If you close Messenger and open another app, people will see this activity

9 Creating and joining events

Don't fear missing out. This chapter looks at how you can receive and manage invites to events. It also shows you how to create events, send invitations and generate some publicity.

Receiving invites to events

Millions of events take place across the world each and every year. There are birthdays to celebrate, weddings to attend and numerous graduations, bachelor and bachelorette parties, launches, openings, leaving drinks, house-warming gatherings, and so much more.

Facebook allows you to create and receive invitations to events. You can then respond to the invitation, indicating whether or not you are likely to attend. Doing so helps event planners work out how many people they need to cater for. Invites can also help spread the word about a public event.

Viewing and responding to an invite

1 When you are invited to an event, you will receive a notification. You can also view the events you are invited to by clicking on the **Events** tab in the left-hand menu of the Facebook website, or by tapping the **Menu** button in the Facebook app and selecting **Events**

2 Any events that you have been invited to will be shown, detailing who has sent the invite. Click on the event to see more details about it. You will be able to see how many other people have stated they are going

3 If the event is public, you can indicate that you are **Interested** or you can state that you are **Going**

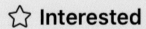

4 If the event is private, the options are different. You will be asked to state whether you are **Going**, considering going (so **Maybe**) or **Can't Go**. An event host will be able to see that you have viewed the invitation

Beware

When you indicate that you are interested in an event or are going, the information will be posted to your Timeline.

Beware

Looked at a private invite? The event creator and the guests who are going will know you have viewed it.

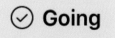

Hot tip

You can change your mind about an event by revisiting it and selecting a different response.

Exploring other events

You don't have to be invited to an event to be able to see what's going on. Facebook will flag up any events taking place near to your location and you will also be able to see events that are proving to be popular among your friends. Facebook will also make suggestions and you'll see online-only events too.

Want to see past events? On the main Events page, click **Calendar** and select **Past Events**.

1 Click the **Events** tab in the left-hand menu of the Facebook website, or open the Facebook app, tap the **Menu** button and select **Events**

2 Scroll down the list of suggested events and see if any are of interest to you

3 At the **Browse Events By** section, you can choose a category and view any events associated with it

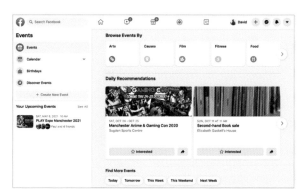

Clicking **Calendar** in the left-hand menu lets you see events by date.

125

4 This will also present you with a list of filters. You can opt to see family-friendly or online events. You can also search by location and time

5 If you spot an event that you'd like to attend, you can click **Interested**. It's a good idea to click its name for more details. Doing so also lets you indicate whether you intend **Going** and you'll be able to see how many have responded and what's likely to take place

6 Don't want to go alone? You can also invite other people by clicking **Invite** and selecting friends who may want to attend too

Hot tip

See the events a friend is already attending by going to their profile, clicking **More** underneath their cover image on the website version, and selecting **Events** (if they have not hidden this section).

Sharing an event

If you want others to join in the fun of a public event, you can share it. At the same time, you are able to limit the number of people who you share it with.

1 Find an event that interests you and select it. It may be an event that you are already attending or one you are simply considering: sharing can help encourage others to go along with you

2 Beneath the profile header on both the Facebook website and the app is a **Share** button. Click it

3 Choose how you want to share. You can:

- **Share as a post or send in Messenger**. These two options are available via the website and the app.

- **Invite friends**. You will see a list of friends. Select **Invite** next to their name (on the website, there is a dedicated **Invite** button so use that for this option).

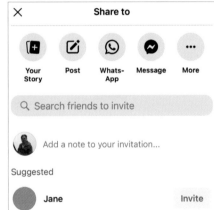

- **Share to your Story**. Do this and the event will appear in your Story for 24 hours.

- **Copy the link**. This will create a URL that you can paste into social media and email.

4 Selecting **More** in Android gives you many extra options, including saving to Drive, Hangouts, Chats and Gmail. In iOS, you can view the built-in Share sheet with options to share via Messages, Mail, Notes, and others

Controlling event invites

You may be attending an event that you don't want others to know about. Perhaps you've been invited but, by expressing you are interested, you risk upsetting those who haven't been asked. Or, maybe you just don't want to promote exactly where you are going to be at a certain point in time in the future.

Hiding your interest in an event

1 To prevent others from knowing that you are interested in attending an event, you can save it instead. Click the three-dot **Menu** button on the page for the event

2 Click or tap **Save**

Blocking somebody from sending you invites

1 For whatever reason, you may not want to receive an invite from a specific person. If this is the case, click the downward-facing arrow in the top-right corner of the screen on Facebook

2 Select **Settings & Privacy** and click **Settings**

3 Select **Blocking** from the left-hand menu

4 Look down the list for **Block event invites** and type in the name of the friend you want to block

Block invites from | Type the name of a friend...

5 Any future event requests from that person will be automatically ignored

Receiving event notifications

Once you have decided you would like to attend an event, you can enjoy receiving notifications about it. You should be kept up-to-date with any changes or discover more about what is going to take place. Notifications often act as a nice reminder about a forthcoming event and they can heighten the level of excitement you feel about attending.

Event notifications appear within the Notifications section of Facebook, and you can access them by selecting the Globe icon on the website and app.

But what if you want the notifications to stop?

Controlling the event notifications

1 Visit the page of the event that you have expressed a positive interest in attending

2 Select the three-dot **Menu** icon (or tap the **More** button in the app)

3 Click or tap **Notification Settings**

4 Choose one of the following four options:

- **All notifications**. Selecting this ensures you receive every notification.

- **Highlights**. You will only see the most important information from the organizers and friends.

- **Host updates only**. Only the information posted by the organizers will be flagged up.

- **Off**. You won't receive any more notifications about the event.

5 Click **Done** on the website or tap the **Back** button in the mobile app

Viewing upcoming birthdays

Facebook will notify you of a friend's birthday as long as they have included the date in their profile. You'll be told ahead of time and on the day. There is a special section within events too.

1 Keep an eye on your notifications, where information about birthdays is flagged up

> It's **Paul's** birthday today.
> Send him good thoughts!   •••
> 34 m

2 To see other birthdays, click **Events** in the left-hand menu. Then, on the Events page on the website, you can select **Birthdays**

3 Recent birthdays (as well as any today) are shown first, allowing you to write a message on their Timeline. Upcoming birthdays are listed next, followed by those in previous months

Managing the details of your own birthday

Your birthday can reveal a lot about you, not least your exact age. If you would prefer people not to know, you can manage what others see while still letting friends wish you a happy birthday. Hiding the full details of your birthday is also a good idea from a privacy and security perspective.

1 Click your profile picture

2 Click **About**

3 Select **Contact and Basic Info** from the left-hand menu

4 Click the **Edit** button to the right of your birthday information. You can then select what is viewable by others. We would suggest making the year you were born visible only to yourself by selecting **Only me**

Hot tip

In some geographical locations, two weeks before your birthday Facebook will send you a message on your News Feed, asking if you want to create a fundraiser. Choose a nonprofit organization, and your friends will be invited to donate money to that particular cause.

The mobile app interface for setting up events is largely similar to that of the website. But you can't choose an illustration for your cover photo via the app.

Keep the name of your Group short to avoid the title of your event being cut when it is displayed.

Creating an event

If you are hosting an event, whether private or public, you too can use Facebook not only to promote it, but also to invite people along.

Getting started

1 Go to the Events page via the left-hand menu in Facebook, and click **+ Create Event**. If you are using the app, go to the Events section and tap **+ Create**

2 Choose between an **Online** or **In Person** event. An online event can be conducted via Messenger Rooms, Facebook Live or a third-party app that allows you to provide an external link. An In Person event is a traditional physical meet-up

Filling in the details of an event
The setup for Online and In Person events is largely the same.

1 Enter the name of the event

2 Select both the start and end dates using the drop-down selection menus. Do the same with the times

3 Indicate who should be able to see and join your event. You can select **Private** and restrict attendance to people you invite (if you choose this, you can decide whether to allow guests to invite their friends). You can also open your event to anyone you are friends with by clicking **Friends**. Events can be restricted to members of a particular Group, too, but if you want as many people as possible to consider attending, make it **Public**. That way your event can be viewed and joined by anyone, whether they are on Facebook or not

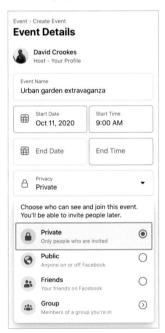

4 Click **Next**

5 For a physical event, you can add a real-life **Location** but for an online event, you can choose between Messenger Rooms or Facebook Live as the location for your event. If you don't want to use either, you can add a link to a different online location by selecting **External Link** or you can choose **Other**, in which case you'll have to tell attendees how they can participate in the event

Cover photos should be 1,200 pixels wide and 628 pixels tall.

6 Click **Upload Cover Photo** and search your computer for a suitable image. Alternatively, select **Choose Illustration** and click a category that best suits your forthcoming event before taking your pick from the good number of pictures available for use. If the viewable part of the image doesn't look right, you can drag the picture to reposition it

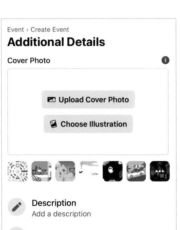

7 Click **Description** and write a compelling overview of your event. This is a great way to sell the event to potential attendees. Click **Save**

8 Click **Event Settings** and you can add friends as co-hosts for your event. You can also opt to show the guest list of people looking to attend. Click **Save**

9 While you've been inputting the event details, they've been updating in the Desktop Preview. If you're happy with what you see, click **Create Event**

131

Sending event invitations

To make people aware of a private event, you will need to invite your friends to it. Friends do not have to be on Facebook to be invited. You can invite people by email and text.

Beware

You can "only" personally invite 500 people to your event. By allowing friends attending the event to also invite people, you can get around this restriction if need be.

1 On the page for your event, click **Invite**

2 Select **Choose Friends**

3 Go down the list of friends and choose people to invite, or enter a phone number or email and select that

4 Any people you add to the invite list will be placed in the third column of the Invite box for a clearer view

5 When you are done, click **Send Invites**

Inviting friends on a mobile device
It's also possible to use the phone or tablet app to send invitations.

1 Select the **Menu** button in the app and tap **Events**. Open the page for your event in the app

2 Tap **Calendar** at the top of the screen and you'll see the events that you're hosting

3 Open the event

4 Tap **Invite**, which is located just under the event banner image

5 Select the people you want to invite

6 Tap **Send Invitation** when you've created a list you're happy with

Managing your event

Once you have created your event, you will want to keep a close eye on who is responding to it.

1 Go to the page for your event

2 Look at the section called **Responses**. This will indicate how many people are **Going** to the event and those who are **Maybe/Interested** and **Invited**

Responses		
Going	Maybe	Invited
0	0	1
✉ Invite Friends		

3 Tap this section for a greater breakdown (or click **See All** if you're using the website). It will show exactly who has decided they will attend and who is wavering

4 You will also be able to see a list of invited people who have indicated that they **Can't go**

Altering the description of the event and adding co-hosts

Should you need to amend your event, Facebook allows you to edit the details you created when you set it up. This is great if, for example, your birthday party has suddenly become a joint celebration, or if you need to clarify a misleading description.

1 Visit the page for your event and click **Edit**

2 Make your amends

3 Click **Update**

Beware

If you decide to add a co-host, then they will be able to edit your event details and invite others.

Hot tip

Facebook doesn't allow you to formally change an event from private to public, but if you select **Duplicate** via the three-dot **More** button on your event listing you can change the privacy setting and resubmit it.

Hot tip

Share a public event on your own Timeline, or in your Group or Page. If you want to spread the word further, ask others to share it as well.

Building some excitement

Don't just set up an event and leave it to chance that people will engage with it. Keep adding content to create a buzz, and encourage others to share it. This is particularly important if your event is a public one.

1 Go to the page of the event you are hosting and click **Add a Post**

2 To write a post, simply type into the section labeled **Write something...**

3 To engage using visuals, click the **Photo** icon in the Create Post box. You can also add a location, tag friends or include a GIF if you wish

4 Click the three-dot **More** button for even more options. Why not click **Poll** and create an engaging survey? You can also raise money for a good cause on your event page

5 Click **Post** when you are finished

Setting up a fundraiser

Want to raise money for a charitable organization or a personal cause? You can do so using Facebook. It's also possible to donate to causes that others have created if and when you see one.

1 Click **See More** in the left-hand menu and select **Fundraisers** (or tap the **Menu** button in the app and find the option there)

2 Click **+ Raise Money** (or tap **+ Create Fundraiser** in the app)

3 Choose between a charity, personal cause, or yourself

4 When selecting **Charity**, choose the nonprofit you wish to support from the list or search manually

5 If selecting a **Personal Cause** or **Yourself** choose a category (Medical, Personal emergency, Family, Business, Pets/animals, Faith or Other)

6 Enter the required information in the boxes to the left of the screen or work your way down the boxes in the app. You'll be asked for the amount of money you want to raise; the currency, end date and title of your fundraiser; as well as a description of why you are raising funds

7 Select a **Cover Photo**

8 Select **Create**. If you have created a personal fundraiser, Facebook's team will need to review it

Cancel	Create fundraiser	Create

CHOOSE A CATEGORY

Category — Personal emergency

NAME YOUR FUNDRAISER

David's personal emergency fundraiser

TELL YOUR STORY

Why are you raising money? How and when will the money be used?

Get help with writing your story

SET A GOAL — See tips and payment info

Goal amount — £200

Canceling and deleting events

If you decide you don't want to go ahead with an event, you can cancel it. Facebook will let you inform all of the guests, and you can choose if you wish to delete everything posted to the event.

1 Click the three-dot **More** button on the page for the event you're hosting

2 Select **Cancel Event**

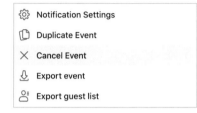

3 You can cancel the event by selecting the button next to **Cancel Event**. You will be able to add a post to the Event page, explaining your decision and what people should do

4 If you select the button next to **Delete Event**, all of the posts will be erased. In both cases, guests will be notified

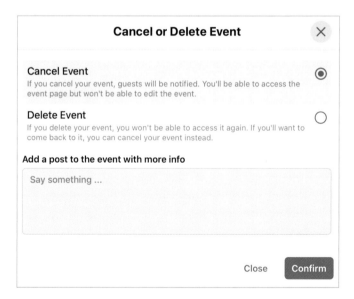

5 Click **Confirm**

6 Note that canceled or deleted events won't be listed under the Past section on the main Event page

10 Using photos and videos

Earlier chapters have touched on how you can upload images and videos to Facebook, but these pages show ways of editing your media and creating albums.

Uploading photos and videos

They've long said a picture paints a thousand words, and that is very much true here. Indeed, photos and videos are a key part of Facebook's appeal. They let you share a snapshot of your life, and they allow you to put funny images and cartoons out there for all to see.

You can find out more about the basics of uploading photos and videos on pages 46 and 47.

1 Click or tap **Photo** or **Photo/Video** in the Create Post box at the top of your News

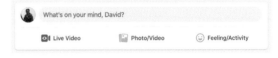

Feed or Timeline, depending on whether you are accessing Facebook on your computer or mobile device

2 Browse for an image or video on your computer or device, selecting any media you want to share with others. Click **Choose**, **Done** or **Next** depending on the device

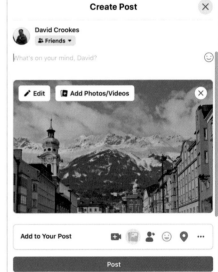

3 Write something

4 If you need to add more images, click **Add Photos/Videos** (on the website). On the app, you can tap the image or video icons to add more

5 Select the drop-down marked **Friends**, and choose who can see your post

6 Tap **Post**

Adding tags to photos

If your image contains people, Facebook will allow you to associate a tag with them. Essentially, this means you are able to put a name to the face, and it's a nice way of identifying who has been photographed while letting the people you have tagged know an image of them has been posted.

1 Upload a photo to Facebook

2 Click the **Edit** button on the image

3 Click **Tag Photo** (or tap the Tag icon if you're using the Facebook app)

4 Click on a face and box will appear. You can type a name or choose from the suggested list of names to associate that person with the image

5 Click **Save** (or **Done**, depending on the device)

6 When anyone views the image, they will be able to see exactly who is pictured. The people included will also be informed they've been tagged

Don't forget

When you tag someone in a photo, the image may appear on their News Feed, depending on their security settings.

Hot tip

Other Facebook users are able to tag you in photos. Find out how to manage and remove them on pages 175 and 178.

Editing your photographs

Facebook has its own image-editing suite. It is nowhere near as sophisticated as dedicated software such as Photoshop, but it will allow you to crop your images and add filters, stickers and text.

1 Upload your photo, hover over it in the Create Post box and click **Edit**   ✏ Edit

2 Facebook's editing suite will then appear on the screen

Cropping your images

Perhaps the most useful editing tool is Crop. It lets you home in on a particular section of your image and remove sections that get in the way. You can also rotate your image here.

1 Click **Crop** from the left-hand menu

2 Click and hold the circles located in the four corners of the image. You're going to move these so that the section of the image you want to retain is of a brighter color than the parts you don't need

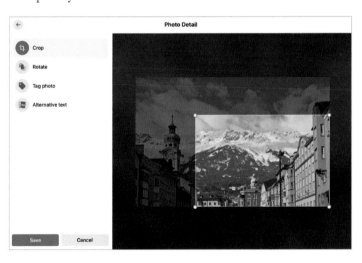

3 When you are satisfied that you've highlighted the section you want to use in your post, click **Save**

4 Click the Back arrow

Hot tip

The cropping function is also available in the app. Select the Crop icon and use the handles in the four corners to highlight the part of the image you wish to keep. In this case, you can also tap **Resize** and choose between the original size or a square. Click **Done** when you're finished.

Rotating the image

1 If you want to flip the image 90 degrees at a time, click **Rotate** when editing an image on the website

2 Keep clicking until it's in the right position and **Save**

3 If you're using the app rather than the website, then the rotate function is within the **Crop** function. Select this and then tap **Rotate**, again continuing to tap until it's in the right position. When you are satisfied with the image, you can tap **Done**

Adding alternative text

1 Adding alternative text is important because it allows people with vision loss to use screen readers to determine the content of your image. Click **Alternative text**

2 You can write your own alternative text or you can check and authorize the description suggested by Facebook

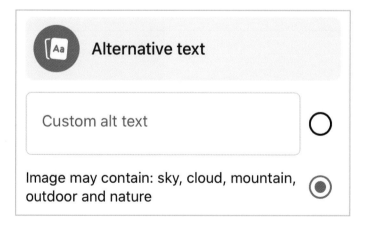

3 Click **Save** when you're finished

...cont'd

Hot tip

You can also overlay GIFs (a moving sticker in this case) and emojis onto your images by selecting those tabs and choosing an appropriate graphic.

Hot tip

An easy way to edit your image is to apply a filter. Click **Effects** in the app's editing screen and you can choose from different looks including Fade, Vintage and Chalk (depending on your device). You can also select frames such as laughing emojis or add effects that can turn any image into a work of art.

Adding stickers

1 Tap the **Stickers** icon in the app

2 Now, tap the Stickers tab and select a sticker

3 Select location, time, temperature, or tag to indicate where and when the image was taken, how hot (or not) it was and to describe the scene. You can also choose a song or indicate feelings

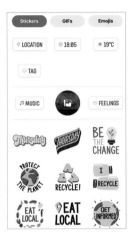

4 The sticker will be overlaid onto your image. Use your fingers to position it

Adding text and drawing

1 To add text over your image, select the **Text** icon

2 Start typing and use the color, justify and font features to alter how your text looks

3 The text will be laid over your image and you can use your fingers to position it

4 To draw on your image, select the **Scribble** icon

5 You get different brushes and a color palette. Use your finger to draw on the image. You can increase the size of your brushes using the slider

Sharing 360-degree photos

In recent years, 360-degree photographs have become very popular since they are more immersive than standard images. Facebook allows you to snap and share these photos on a mobile device. Viewers can then look around the virtual environments, either by dragging a finger around the screen or by moving the device.

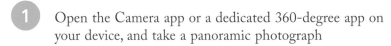

Hot tip

You see lots of samples of 360-degree content on the Facebook 360 Community page at https://www.facebook.com/groups/facebook360community

1 Open the Camera app or a dedicated 360-degree app on your device, and take a panoramic photograph

2 Open the Facebook app and in the Create Post box, select **Photo/Video**. Choose the image you wish to share

3 When you tap **Post**, the 360-degree shot will be available to view

4 Others can then view the image by moving their finger around the screen. A Compass icon will appear on the image to show that it was taken in 360 degrees. The device's gyroscope will also allow you to move the device around to see more of the photo. You can use your mouse if you are viewing the content on your computer

Creating a panoramic shot

Your device has to be capable of creating a 360-degree or panoramic photo. There are 360-enabled cameras on the market but your phone may be powerful enough. Any iPhone 4S or newer, for instance, or Samsung Galaxy S5 or newer, can do it.

Converting your image into 3D

You can add a fantastic 3D effect to any photo that you post on Facebook. This creates the illusion of depth.

1　Launch the Facebook app on your iOS or mobile device and tap **Photo** into the Create post box

2　Search through your Camera Roll for an image or take a fresh photo by tapping the Camera icon

3　Tap **Done** (or **Next**)

4　At the top of your image, you'll see an option called **Make 3D** or **3D Photo**

5　When you tap this, your device will quickly process the image and create a 3D version of it

6　Move your device around and you'll see the 3D effect in action. If you like the result, you can add extra information if you wish and tap **Post**

Creating an album

As well as uploading a single photo or even a series of videos, you can also create and group them within an album.

1 Click your profile image at the top-right corner of Facebook page

2 Click **Photos**

3 Select **+ Create Album**

4 Fill in the boxes in the left column with the album name and an optional description

5 Click **Upload Photos or Videos** and select images from your computer to begin to build your album

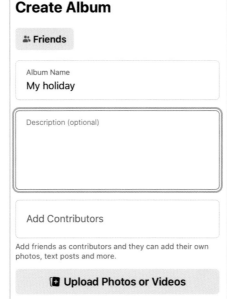

Create Album

👥 Friends

Album Name
My holiday

Description (optional)

Add Contributors

Add friends as contributors and they can add their own photos, text posts and more.

⊕ Upload Photos or Videos

6 Determine who should see your album by clicking the **Friends** button and deciding if it should be made public, available to your friends on Facebook, limited to a specific set of people or whether certain users should be excluded

7 If you want the album to be for your eyes only, then select **Only Me**

8 Click **Post**

Hot tip

Why not let friends add their own images to your album? Click **Add contributors** in the Create Album window and enter their names.

Hot tip

Click your profile image and select **Photos** to see your albums.

Facebook Watch has more than 1.25 billion visitors every month so you're in good company.

Enjoying videos using Watch

Facebook has a built-in video viewer called Watch. It's packed with entertainment so, if you're at a loose end, you can kick back and discover what is currently on offer. It is also possible to enjoy Watch in the company of friends and family, and you can even view Watch on your television.

Viewing on the website

1   Click the **Watch** icon, which you'll see at the top of the screen

2   You'll see a selection of suggested videos. Scroll down the screen and watch any you like the look of. You can also find **Shows** and **Live** broadcasts using the options in the left-hand menu

3   Any videos you enjoy can be saved by clicking the three-dot menu in the top-left corner and selecting **Save video**. These will appear in the Saved Videos category in the left-hand menu

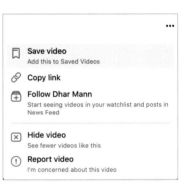

4   There are also options to copy a link, follow the creator, hide the video if you don't like it or report it if there are any issues

Viewing on the app

1   Tap the **Watch** icon

2   Tap the categories at the top of the screen and scroll down to view videos. You can save them, follow the creator, hide the video or give feedback

3   Tap the **Profile** button to view saved videos and history

Creating a Watch Party

Rather than view videos on your own, why not invite others to watch with you in real time? It is possible to start a Watch Party from your News Feed.

1 Click **What's on your mind** to create a post

2 Click the three-dot menu **Menu** button within Add to Your Post and select **Watch Party**

3 Search for videos either manually or by working your way through the tabs, looking

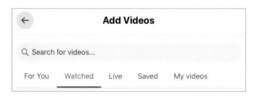

at suggested playlists, videos watched, those that are live, saved or your own. Select those you want to watch with others and click **Next**

4 Write a description if you wish and click **Post**

5 The Watch Party will be posted on your Timeline and others will see it in their News Feed. It is possible to invite friends using the Share button and write comments as you watch. More videos can be viewed by clicking **Add Video**

Hot tip

When you're ready to bring a Watch Party to a close, tap the three-dot **Menu** button in the top-right corner of the video and select **End Watch Party**. Videos from a completed Watch Party are saved in a post on your Timeline along with any comments.

147

Enjoying Facebook Watch on your television

Many smart televisions and TV streaming devices give you access to the Facebook Watch TV app. You will have to visit the App Store on your TV or streaming platform but devices include relatively new Samsung TVs, Amazon Fire TV, Apple TV and Android TV. It is also possible to view Watch on Facebook Portal. See Chapter 7 for more details about Facebook Portal.

Broadcasting live videos

Facebook Live has proven to be very popular, allowing you to broadcast videos in real time. You can create a live broadcast from your computer or phone.

Hot tip

You can view live broadcasts when they appear in your News Feed or through Facebook Watch. You can also visit **https://www.facebook.com/watch/live/**

Hot tip

If you are watching a video on Facebook and you are deaf or hard of hearing, you may be able to view closed captions. With Facebook on your computer, click the downward arrow in the top-right corner, select **Settings & Privacy**, tap **Settings**, select **Videos** and use the drop-down menu next to turn **Always Show Captions** to On.

1 Click **Live Video** in the Create Post box on your computer. Or, tap **Live** on the app

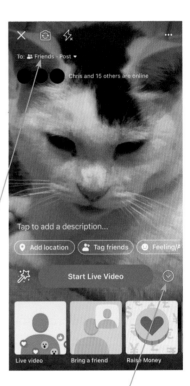

2 Allow access to your camera and microphone, and choose the camera you want to use (either front or back on a mobile device)

3 Describe your live video and decide if you want to add a location, tag friends or indicate a feeling

4 Select who should be able to see your broadcast by tapping the **Friends** drop-down menu

5 In the app, you can make use of effects by tapping the downward arrow at the bottom of the screen in iOS or the **+** in Android. There are props that can be placed over your face and an option to broadcast with a friend (simply choose the friend you want to broadcast with)

6 Click **Go Live** to begin broadcasting from the website or tap **Start Live Broadcast**

7 Your friends will be notified that they can tune in to watch you

11 Buying and selling

Although the likes of eBay and Gumtree are very popular online marketplaces, this chapter explores using Facebook as a way of selling your items and potentially picking up a bargain.

Facebook does not take a cut of any money spent on Marketplace.

Purchases made on Marketplace are not protected by Facebook.

Introducing Marketplace

As well as allowing you to keep up to speed with what your friends are doing, and to message and join groups, Facebook also lets you buy and sell items. You can:

- Discover the items that people close by have listed for sale.

- Narrow down your searches by category, location or price.

- Learn more about the various sellers and communicate with them by direct message.

Using Marketplace is a great way to make some money after having a clear-out and, since items tend to be cheaper than in the shops, it is a lovely way of saving some cash too. Many people use it to look for items that are unavailable in the shops, and it is rapidly growing in popularity.

Opening Marketplace on a mobile device
To open Marketplace on a smartphone or tablet:

1 Ensure that you have the latest version of the Facebook app installed so that you will have the most up-to-date version of Marketplace that's available

2 Tap the Marketplace icon, which you will see either at the top or bottom of the screen, depending on the mobile version that you are using

Opening Marketplace on a computer
The larger screen of a PC or Mac makes it easier for you to see the items you are thinking about buying.

1 Go to **facebook.com** in a browser and log in

2 Click **Marketplace** in the left-hand menu

3 You will be taken to the Marketplace Home screen, from where you will be able to browse the items that are on offer and sell something of your own

What can you buy?

Since it launched, Marketplace has become a bustling emporium with many items across a host of categories being traded each day. Check out the category list for a flavor.

Paying for items bought, and receiving cash for items sold

If you have ever bought or sold an item online, then it's likely you will have done so using eBay. This service relies, to a great extent, on the online payment service PayPal, which lets users send and receive cash quickly and easily without needing to divulge any actual payment card details.

With Facebook Marketplace, you and a seller (or you and a buyer) are left to sort out the payment details yourself.

You could use PayPal but there is no automatic link from the Marketplace for such a service, so you have to go direct to **paypal.com** or use the PayPal app. Alternatively, you could try other online payment services, or arrange a personal visit and complete the transaction with cash.

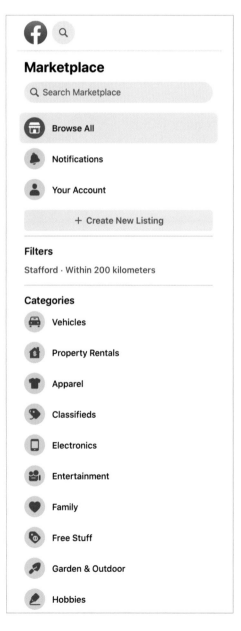

Beware

Don't send money to someone online unless you are 100 per cent confident the person is trustworthy. Facebook advises face-to-face Marketplace transactions.

151

Discovering items for sale

If you are looking for an item to buy on Facebook Marketplace, there are various features to help you to find what you are after. These allow you to search for something specific, or else browse according to the category that best takes your fancy.

Finding Marketplace items on a mobile

Hot tip

When a seller reduces the price of an item, this will be flagged up clearly in the listings, helping you to identify some potential bargains.

Search Marketplace. By tapping the Search icon, you are able to type in a search query.

Category button. Tap this to call up a list of categories and sub-categories, ranging from Home and Entertainment to Hobbies and Family.

Notifications show any items being sold by friends and Groups. Items you have viewed will be flagged here too.

Location button. By default, Marketplace will show items based on your current location. You can change this by tapping it.

Listings. Each of these images represents a product

you can buy from another Marketplace user. To see more listings, simply scroll down the screen, and they will appear.

Note that while the screen above has been taken from the iOS version, the features are the same for Android.

Finding Marketplace items on a computer

Search Marketplace. If you need to search for a specific item, use this bar.

Browse All button. Clicking this will let you see the items that are currently on sale.

Filters. Change the location, set minimum and maximum prices, and determine condition.

You can set your location from as close as 1 km away to as far as 500 km away via the location filter.

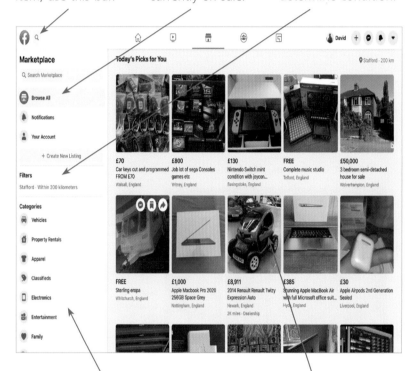

Category buttons. Click on the categories, and they will expand to show you a number of sub-categories. Each helps to narrow your search further.

Listings. These entries show an image of the product, the price, a brief description, the time of posting, and the item's location.

Setting a specific price bracket for searches

1. Click a category to see the **Price** filter

2. Select a minimum and maximum price

3. The listings will change accordingly

153

Examining the product pages

If you see two or more dots at the bottom of an image (or a selection of thumbnail images), it means there is more than one photo available. Scroll or click to see them all.

Each item listed on Facebook's Marketplace contains the same vital information that will help you to make an informed purchasing decision:

- A description of the item, including a photograph.

- The location from which it is being sold, including a map.

- When it was uploaded to Marketplace.

- The price at which it is being sold.

- Options to save or share the item.

- Its state: i.e. whether or not it is new and boxed.

- The profile image and name of the seller.

- An option to message the seller.

Keep an eye out for sellers who are marked as being **Very Responsive**. Since they typically reply to messages within an hour, you may enjoy a less troublesome transaction.

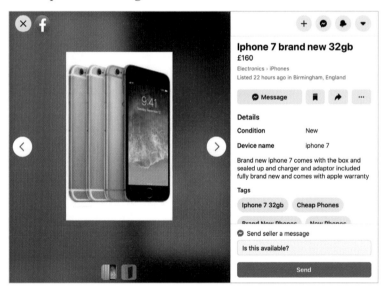

Checking the seller

Click or tap on the seller's name and you will be able to check when they joined Facebook and look at how many items they have for sale. You will also be able to view their profile.

Such steps will assist you in vetting a seller before you make the necessary arrangements toward purchasing an item from Facebook's Marketplace.

Sending sellers a message

If you like the look of an item but you need more information, you can send the seller a direct message.

Using the app

1 Click or tap the item you want to buy on the listing page

2 Tap the box at the bottom of the screen that says **Is this still available?**

3 Either leave the message as it is or delete that text and write your own. You could ask about the condition of the item, whether or not the seller delivers, or simply express an interest in buying

4 Tap **Send**

Using a computer

1 Click the item you like the look of and steer your eyes toward the right-hand panel where you will see a section that says **Is this available?**

2 Either use those words or write your own

3 When you are happy with the message, tap **Send**

4 Now, sit back and wait for a reply

Avoid sharing any financial information in your message, and don't give out your email address or phone number to a seller.

After you have messaged the seller, keep an eye on your notifications for a reply.

Creating your own item post

Do you have some items that you would like to sell? You can quickly create your own post on Marketplace.

Using the app

1 Tap **Sell**

2 You can list an item, vehicle or properties for sale or rent. We're assuming **Items**

3 Tap **Add Photos** to access the images stored on your device. You can also tap the Camera icon on this screen to take a fresh image

4 Fill in the form with the item title and price. Choose a category, indicate the condition and check your location. Describe the item. More detail increases the chance of selling

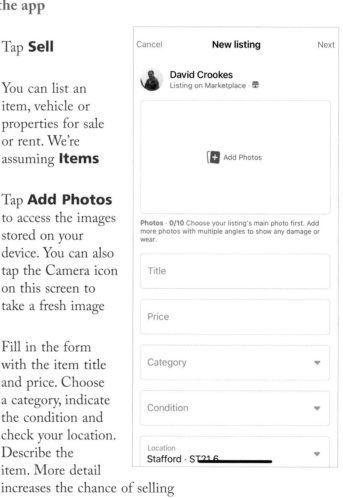

5 Add tags to make the item easier to find

6 Decide if you're offering delivery. You can also hide the item from your friends. This prevents listing in a Group

7 Tap **Next** and decide where you want to list the item

8 Tap **Publish**

Using the website

1 Click **+ Create New Listing**

2 Select a listing type. You can choose to sell an item in a single category, sell a vehicle, or put a property up for sale or rent. Assuming you're selling an item, click **Item for Sale**

3 Use the form to the left of the Preview screen to add a photo from your computer and input the item's title, price, category and condition. Describe the item and add up to 20 tags. The Preview screen will constantly update

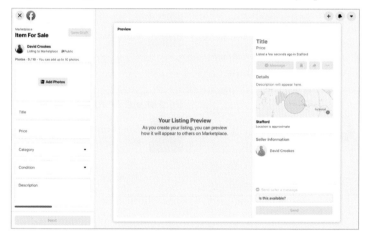

4 Check your location is correct and determine if you're listing as a single item or if you have more than one item in stock

5 Click **Next**

6 Marketplace items will be made public. You can also list the item in up to 20 Groups

7 When you are happy with your listing, click **Publish**

Keeping track of items you sell

Once you have listed your items, you will need to keep track of them. Marketplace makes it easy to see which of your items are available and which have sold, and it brings all of the messages relating to your items into one place.

1 Tap the Marketplace profile button

2 Tap **Your listings** under the Selling section

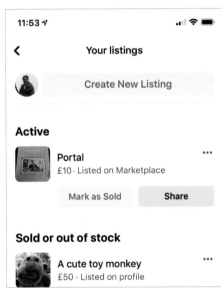

3 Those listed under **Active** are still available to buy. You'll see a thumbnail image of the item, its title and the price

4 You will see a section dedicated to messages from potential buyers. You can view and reply to them

Marking an item as sold

When you sell an item, you have to manually mark it as having been sold. It's a good idea to do this because it removes the item from sale, and it also makes it easy to see which items you still need to sell.

1 Underneath each item listing, you will see an option for **Mark as Sold**. Tap it

2 You can, if you wish, reverse this by selecting **Mark as Available** at a later date. To do so, tap the three-dot (...) menu next to the listing and choose this option

Editing your item listings

Have you made a mistake with your listing? Do you need to remove it? Or, would you like to post it to somewhere else as well? You can do all of these things.

1 Tap the Marketplace profile button

2 Tap **Your listings** under the section Selling

3 Tap the three-dot **Menu** button next to the item that you want to edit

4 Select **Edit listing** and review before publishing again

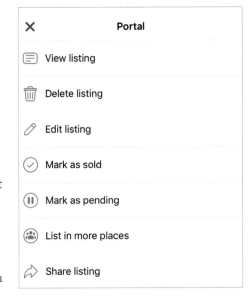

✕	Portal
🗏	View listing
🗑	Delete listing
✎	Edit listing
✓	Mark as sold
⏸	Mark as pending
👥	List in more places
➢	Share listing

Hot tip

You can use as many as 10 photos in your listings, so don't hold back.

Keeping track of items and editing on the website

You are also able to monitor the items you are selling on the Marketplace website.

1 Tap **Your listings** in the left-hand menu

2 This will activate a page that splits your items into **Active** and **Sold**

The website lets you delete, edit and repost listings too. This is good news for anyone who prefers to work on a larger screen.

Deleting a listing

When you delete a listing, you are asked to specify why. Let Facebook know if you ended up selling the item on Facebook or elsewhere, or whether or not it's still available. You can, however, opt not to answer.

Beware

Bear in mind that some people would avoid listings that are littered with poor grammar and spelling mistakes.

Getting a good price for items

Whether you are buying or selling, you'll want to pay or receive a good price for items. Here are some tips:

- **Be prepared for negotiation**. If you are buying an item, don't be afraid to put in an offer that is less than the asking price. The seller can only say no. Similarly, be open to people asking for your items for less. One way to combat this is to price your items a little bit higher. Not so high that it puts people off from buying, though.

- **Get the images right**. Photos sell an item, so make sure that any you take

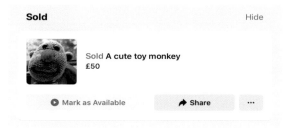

are sharp and showcase the item well. That means ditching blurred images and taking a few of them against clean backgrounds in a good light. Poor images will usually result in lower offers, so why not take advantage of that if you see a listing accompanied by a bad photo?

- **Check the description**. Selling an item? Then go into detail so that a buyer can be confident that they know what they will be getting. A good description that covers every question you can think of can also prevent you from being bombarded by quizzical buyers. Buying an item? Then look carefully at what you're getting, and ensure you'll receive value for money.

- **Pay with cash**. Never send cash in the post or wire money to a stranger. But do consider meeting with a buyer or seller and using cash rather than an online payment service. Companies such as PayPal are secure and convenient, but there may be fees involved. Cash transactions can save money for both buyers and sellers. Perhaps offer a discount if someone is willing to pay with notes and coins, and ask for one if you're buying in this way.

- **Stay safe**. You can't put a price on personal safety, so if you meet up with someone you have met on Marketplace, do so in a crowded public place.

12 Tailoring the adverts

Facebook is funded by advertising, but you can change the settings to determine what you do and don't get to see.

Accessing the advert settings

Facebook is free to use but, since it has to be paid for in some way, it may not be surprising to learn that advertising brings in the bulk of the social network's revenue.

This is no bad thing. Facebook is, after all, a very useful service and its adverts are mostly unobtrusive. But you should still keep a check on the adverts that are being served to you.

How are advertisers targeting you?

Facebook is attractive to advertisers because they are able to tap into data about the network's users. It allows businesses to target you with adverts that are relevant not only to the things you like, but also the area in which you live, your age, your gender, and more. This increases the chance of you engaging with an advertiser and, you never know, you may see something you like.

As you can guess, much of this relies on the information that you are "giving away" on the social network. When you click Like on a post, for instance, check in at a location or use the mobile app, Facebook can get a more rounded view of you.

And yet it's important to note that Facebook is not being sinister. It is transparent about what it collects and does with your data, and it is clear about what it won't do (it won't read your emails, for instance).

Still, Facebook's reach can be wide. Businesses can install code on their websites that records when you visit, or cross-reference the email or phone number you use on Facebook with any records they have themselves.

Visiting the advertising settings on Facebook

1. Click the downward arrow in the top-right corner

2. Select **Settings & Privacy**

3. Click **Settings**

4. Click **Ads** in the left-hand menu

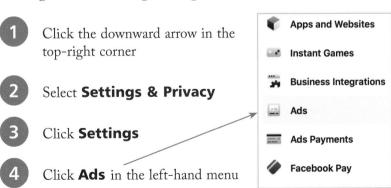

Configuring your interests

The first section you will see is Your interests. It is made up of items gathered as you make use of Facebook. For example, liking a page related to the Victorian era created an entry in this section for that very subject. Liking a page related to cats produced an entry for felines. Looking at what Facebook thinks you are interested in should be your first port of call.

1 Click **Your interests**

2 Go through the various categories, which can range from Business and industry to Food and drink. Click **More** to see extra categories

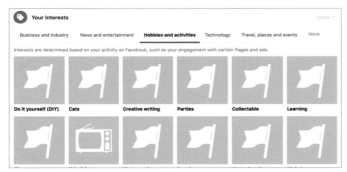

3 Hover over a subject, and it will tell you why

> **About Photography**
> You have this preference because of your activity on Facebook related to Photography's Page, for example clicking on one of their ads.

the preference is listed. In our case, we apparently clicked an advert related to Photography

4 When you hover, you will also see an **X**. Clicking this will remove that particular interest

5 You can click **See More** to view extra interests

You removed

6 You can also indicate whether or not you found the interests section helpful by clicking **Yes** or **No**

Seeing who you've engaged with

Hot tip

Whenever you engage with an advertiser, Facebook makes a note of it, allowing other advertisers with a similar remit to potentially send ads your way. Again, to ensure that the information Facebook has about you is accurate, you should check the data that has been gathered.

1 Click **Advertisers and Businesses**

2 There are three categories of advertiser to click on:

- Those you have interacted with using your contact information. This means the email or phone number you are using on Facebook is included on the customer list of a business.

- Those whose websites or app you have used. This relates to advertisers you have actively engaged with that make use of Facebook technology.

- Those whose ads you have clicked.

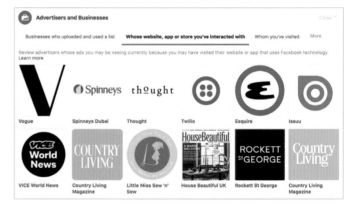

3 For the first category, identify a business and click **View Controls**. You can disallow businesses showing ads using a list or stop them excluding you from ads using a list

4 If an **X** is displayed when you hover over an entry, you can click to **Remove** that business. If you see a downward arrow, you can select **Report** to report the advertiser, or **Hide** to hide any adverts from them

Checking your personal info

Advertisers can make use of information contained on your profile, but you can determine what can and cannot be used.

1 Click **Your information**

2 Click **About you**

3 You will see that Facebook advertisers can make use of your relationship status, employer, job title and education. Next to entries for these is a slider that you can turn on or off (blue for on). Decide what you want advertisers to have access to

4 Click **Your categories**

5 Information obtained by Facebook through your use of the site is shown. It can include your mobile network, Wi-Fi usage or a recent device change. Hover over each entry for more details

6 Remove any details by hovering the mouse over the item, then clicking **X** next to each entry

Beware

As Facebook itself explains, any amendments made to your information under **About you** does not mean the details are hidden from view.

Hot tip

You can also click the downward arrow at the top of the Facebook screen, select **Settings & Privacy** and click **Privacy Checkup**. Selecting **Your ad preferences on Facebook** shows you the settings in Step 3 and lets you determine the setting in Step 4 on page 166.

Altering your advert settings

Here, we are looking at a section that asks you three questions with the aim of making the adverts work better for you.

1 Click **Ad settings**

2 The first question asks whether you would like to see adverts based on your use of websites and apps. This is relevant because Facebook allows websites and apps to use its tracking software, and those that do are able to gather data that the social network can then use to work out which ads are most relevant for you. There are benefits: if you were looking for a new phone, you may see adverts on Facebook promoting good deals. But if you want to turn this off, click **Allowed**, select **Choose Settings** and click **Not allowed**. Reverse this process to activate it again

3 The next question asks if you want to see ads on apps and websites from Facebook Companies. This allows the information gathered about you on Facebook, and from companies that use its tracking software, to display adverts on websites and apps that are not linked to the social network. If you want to turn this off, select **Allowed**, click the drop-down box and click **Not allowed**. Again, reverse this process to reactivate it

4 Finally, you will be asked if you want others to see "adverts with your social actions". This means your friends will see adverts from companies you have liked, shared and commented on (such as in the image here). Adverts will also depend on the events you join and your app usage. If you don't want anyone to see adverts based on how you interact with a particular business, select **Only my friends**, click the drop-down box, and select **No One**. Reverse this to reactivate

Using another ad opt-out

As well as altering the settings on Facebook itself, you are also able to opt out of seeing interest-based advertising from Facebook in your current browser.

1 Go to **http://optout.aboutads.info** to access the website of the Digital Advertising Alliance (DAA) and ensure that you have cookies enabled

2 It will perform a check of your browser before showing you a list of companies participating in the DAA's WebChoices tool. The companies marked **Yes** will have customized ads enabled on your browser

3 Look down the list for Facebook. Click **+** to see more information and, to stop it from customizing ads on your browser, tick the box to the right. You can, if you wish, click **Opt Out Of All** at the bottom of the screen

4 Click **Submit your choices**

Hiding advertisements from view
Seeing an advert you'd rather not view? Tell Facebook.

1 Click the three-dot **Menu** button on an ad

2 Select **Hide ad**

3 You can also select **Report ad** or even save the link or turn on notifications. It'll tell you why you're seeing the ad too

Watching out for fakes

Facebook does all it can to keep you safe, and it will never knowingly serve you fake advertisements. Sometimes, though, a rogue ad may slip through the net and there have been cases of domain names being spoofed to mislead you into clicking; the aim being to direct you to a different website.

You may also see spoof offers that are unwittingly shared by others. Facebook will block all such offenders, but be wary too.

Spotting fakes

The image on this page was not placed as an advert but it fooled some people into sharing it. Those behind it hoped people would click. Websites, however, can contain viruses, or look to trick you into revealing your details. Not everything is quite what it seems.

Hot tip

If an advert directs you to a different website than the one advertised, immediately close the browser tab.

168

Encouraging offer. This UK supermarket was said to be giving £45 vouchers to everyone to celebrate its anniversary. That's a lot of money, and alarm bells should have started ringing straightaway.

No date. Vouchers usually have an expiry date tucked away in the Terms and Conditions. Not this one.

Low-res image. The image is blurry, which isn't very professional.

Bad grammar. A genuine offer (or news story about an offer) would at least get the grammar right. The initial capital of "Everyone" with the accompanying exclamation mark looks suspicious.

Odd website address. Lidl's website is lidl.co.uk This website fails to match that, and it looks strange with its jumble of numbers and letters and a .us suffix. Even if it is a "news story" about the coupon, it looks odd.

13 Privacy and security

If you are concerned that your personal life is being overly exposed on Facebook, then this chapter looks at the various ways you are able to maintain your privacy.

You should also consider the privacy of others in the posts you create.

You can visit **https://www.facebook.com/safety** to learn more about keeping children safe online.

Keeping your privacy intact

Facebook is a social network that encourages you to share your thoughts, day-to-day activities, likes and interests. As such, many people have expressed concerns about privacy and there has been, in recent times, a noticeable fall in the number of users making posts about their own life.

To address this and to continue making the network a personal experience, Facebook has worked on ways of making it easier for you to control your level of privacy. Before we look at those, however, you should consider some common-sense steps for an easier and more private online life.

● Always remember that anything you post on Facebook is typically shared with a wide group of people, some of whom may not be your closest friends. If you wouldn't share something publicly in the real world, think carefully about sharing it on social media.

● It is possible for anyone to take a screenshot. So even if you post something you later regret, deleting it may not solve the issue. Anyone who has taken a screenshot could share it. Again, this comes back to thinking carefully about what you are posting before you press that button.

● Be wary of giving away too much about your whereabouts. You may want to share those pictures of yourself on holiday while you are away or tell all that you're at a concert, but security experts would suggest you wait until you get back. Burglars have been known to keep an eye on Facebook.

● Similarly, don't brag about new purchases or your possessions, and keep a close eye on the personal details you have listed on the site. Are you giving too much away: the name of your school or date of birth, perhaps? Such information can be used for identity fraud or to get past online security questions.

● Consider your reputation. Think about what you are sharing, posting and liking, and how others may view you for doing so. Employers often look at social media to get an indication of your character. Your views may not necessarily tally with those they hold, regardless of where on the political spectrum you may be, or the opinions you hold.

Taking a privacy checkup

The quickest way to keep an eye on your privacy settings is to use Facebook's Privacy Checkup feature. It guides you through some settings so that you can determine what works best for you.

1 Click the downward arrow in the top-right corner of Facebook, and select **Settings & Privacy**

2 Click **Privacy Checkup**

3 You will be shown five options:

- Who can see what you share (page 172).

- How to keep your account secure (page 179).

- How people can find you on Facebook (page 173).

- Your data settings on Facebook (page 185).

- Your ad preferences on Facebook (pages 165-167).

Hot tip

Go to your **About** page to look at more things that Facebook knows about you. Click **Edit** next to the entries if you wish to alter them.

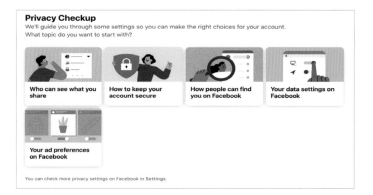

Privacy Checkup
We'll guide you through some settings so you can make the right choices for your account. What topic do you want to start with?

Who can see what you share

How to keep your account secure

How people can find you on Facebook

Your data settings on Facebook

Your ad preferences on Facebook

You can check more privacy settings on Facebook in Settings.

4 Each one will open a guide that presents the various settings you are able to alter

5 Some parts will also assess whether or not you need to take action and suggest what you should do

Controlling who sees your posts

There are some basic privacy settings that you need to take a look at to make sure they work well for you.

1 Follow Steps 1 and 2 on page 171 and select **Who can see what you share**

2 Click **Continue** and review your information

3 Select **Only me** next to each entry to make a change

4 You have four main options:

- **Public** allows anyone to see the information.

- **Friends** ensures only your contacts see it.

- **Only me** keeps the info private.

- **Your custom list** limits the info to a specific list of friends, assuming you have such a list.

5 Select which best suits you for each entry and click **Next**

6 Now, determine who can see your **Future Posts**. Here, as well as choosing Public, Friends and Only Me, you can select **Friends except...** to exclude certain people or select **Specific friends** if you want to limit the viewing to a few chosen contacts. In this case, you'll be asked to pick which friends you want to share with

7 Decide who sees your **Stories**. Click the option button and choose between **Public**, **Friends** or a **Custom list**

8 Even if the public or friends of friends can see your current posts, you can prevent them viewing past posts by clicking **Limit**

9 Click **Next** and you can prevent specific people interacting with your Timeline. Click **Add to Blocked List** and type the names of people you want to block

Configuring who can see you

Facebook also allows you to determine who is able to contact you and who is able to look you up.

1 Follow Steps 1 and 2 on page 171 and select **How people can find you on Facebook**

2 Click **Continue**

3 Configure **Who can send you friend requests?** by clicking the box next to this option. You can limit it to **Friends of friends** if you wish

4 You can also:

- **View pending friend requests**. In each case, select Confirm or Delete and click Next when done.

- **Decide who can look you up using the phone number or email you provided**. People can search for you by inputting your phone number into the Search bar. Choose Everyone, Friends or Friends of friends. Select Only Me to prevent anyone else using this method.

- **Determine if search engines outside of Facebook can link to your profile**. This is unticked by default, so only click it if you don't mind search engines such as Google being able to link to your profile in their results.

Beware

Your profile image and cover photo are always public, since they are used to help others find you on Facebook.

173

Controlling and reviewing posts

It is also important to check what others can add to your Timeline and who is able to view what is posted on there. By changing the settings, you can exert greater control and give yourself the ultimate say over what appears. This can prevent others from posting embarrassing things as well as items that breach your privacy.

Hot tip

Make good use of these settings: they can prevent you from being tagged in embarrassing photos, for example.

1 Click the downward arrow in the top-right corner, click **Settings & Privacy** and select **Settings**

2 Click **Timeline and Tagging** from the left-hand menu

Determining who can add stuff to your Timeline
The first section lets you decide who can post to your Timeline, and whether or not you want to review those posts before they appear for others to see.

1 Click **Edit** next to **Who can post on your timeline?** then click the audience selector. By choosing **Only me** you are able to prevent others from posting to your Timeline

Beware

You can't stop people sharing your posts unless you set them to **Only me** (which means only you would get to see them!).

2 Do the same for **Who can see what others post on your timeline?**

3 You can prevent people from sharing your posts to their Stories. If this is something you want to do, click **Edit** next to **Allow others to share your posts to their stories?** and click **Enabled**. Change this to **Disabled** if you wish

Hot tip

If you are hiding comments containing certain words, enter them in the box that appears or enter them in a spreadsheet, save the file as .CSV and use the Upload function to import them.

4 Click **Edit** next to **Hide comments containing certain words from your timeline** if there are words, phrases or emojis you don't want to see

Selecting what others can see

In this section, you are able to review what others see on your Timeline, and control who sees posts you've been tagged in and who can see what others post. These latter two options are particularly useful if you are allowing anyone to post to your Timeline without checks.

Only you and your friends can potentially post to your Timeline.

1 Click **Edit** next to **Who can see posts you've been tagged in on your timeline?** and make a choice from the audience selector. Selecting **Only me** will ensure any posts you are tagged in are hidden

2 Click **Edit** next to **When you're tagged in a post, who do you want to add to the audience of the post if they can't already see it?** and make a choice from the audience selector. Again, selecting **Only me** will ensure any posts you are tagged in are hidden

Managing tags people add

1 If someone adds a tag to a post, it allows the person tagged and their friends to see the post. To stop these posts automatically appearing on your Timeline, click **Edit** next to **Review posts you're tagged in before the post appears on your timeline?** and select **Enabled**. You'll now be able to review the post first

2 Click **View as** next to **Review what other people see on your timeline** and you'll be shown exactly how your profile looks to other people. Don't like what you see? Then seek out the tagging settings that best suit your preferences

3 When someone adds a tag to one of your posts, you can ensure that you get a say in whether that becomes viewable. Click **Edit** next to **Who sees tag suggestions when photos that look like you are uploaded?** and make your choice

Click **Edit List** next to Restricted List if you want to unblock people. Simply click on their names again.

Blocking users and apps

If you don't want certain friends to see your posts or if you want to block invites, Pages and apps, you can easily manage this on the Manage Blocking page.

1 Click the downward arrow in the top-right corner, click **Settings & Privacy** and select **Settings**

2 Click **Blocking** from the left-hand menu

What you can manage

- **Restricted List**: You can add friends to a Restricted List, which means they will only see your Public posts or items posted on a mutual friend's Timeline. Click **Edit List** next to **Restricted List**, and either search for people or select Friends from the drop-down menu, and click the names of those you want to add to it.

- **Block users**: You can block specific people and prevent them from interacting with you, except in Groups where you are both members. Include the name or email address of people you want to ban in the **Block Users** section, and click **Block**.

  Block users [Type a name] [Block]

- **Block messages, app invites and event invites**: You will see three sections marked

  Block invites from [Type the name of a friend...]

  Block messages, **Block app invites** and **Block event invites**. Type the name of a friend into any of these boxes to block someone from performing the action.

- **Block apps and Pages**: Type the name of an app or Page into the box within the sections for **Block apps** and **Block Pages**, and the apps will not be able to grab non-public information about you or contact you, while the Pages will be unable to interact with your posts or comments. By doing this, you'd automatically unfollow and unlike a Page.

Enhancing mobile privacy

Since you are likely to use Facebook on your mobile rather heavily, you should configure the settings on your device for better privacy.

Better privacy in iOS

1 Tap the **Settings** app from your iOS device's Home screen

2 Keep scrolling until you see the entry for **Facebook**. Tap it

3 Select **Settings**

4 Go down the list of things that Facebook is allowed to access. Move the green sliders to off if you want to stop Facebook accessing that particular feature. You can stop Facebook accessing your Photos, Microphone and Camera. You can also stop the app refreshing in the background, and prevent it from using your mobile data and sending you notifications

Turning off Location will prevent Facebook from sharing your whereabouts when you post something.

Better privacy in Android

1 Tap the **Settings** app

2 Tap **Apps & Notifications** then select **App info**

3 Select **Facebook** and tap **Permissions**

4 Toggle the switches to turn them on and off, as with iOS in Step 4 above

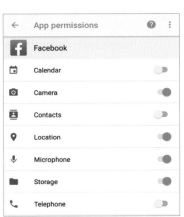

Removing tags from photos

If you allow yourself to be tagged by others, you may end up being tagged in a photo or post that you'd rather wasn't flagged up in such a way. You can remove the tags very easily.

1 Click the downward arrow in the top-right corner of the screen

2 Select **Settings & Privacy** then click **Activity Log**

3 Select **Tag Review** from the left-hand menu

4 Go down the list to find images and posts that you want to be untagged from

5 Select the downward arrow to the right of a post, and click **Remove tag**

6 The tag will then be removed

7 You may also feel that the post in which you were included is offensive in some way. If this is the case, then go through the same steps 1 to 4 as above, but click **Find support or report post**

8 You will then be asked to explain why you are reporting the post. Select the reason and select **Continue**, filling in any other forms that Facebook asks for

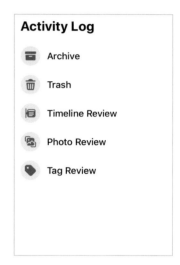

Activity Log

- Archive
- Trash
- Timeline Review
- Photo Review
- Tag Review

Save post

Remove tag
You won't be tagged in this post anymore.

Snooze Frank for 30 days
Temporarily stop seeing posts.

Unfollow Frank
Stop seeing posts but stay friends.

Find support or report post
I'm concerned about this post.

Adding extra login security

As well as changing your password often, you should consider adding two-factor authentication. This means, in addition to using a password, you are sent a code to your phone that you also have to input. It helps prevent anyone else from logging in, since they'd need to know your login details and have possession of your phone.

1 Click the downward arrow in the top-right corner of the screen, select **Settings & Privacy** then **Settings**

2 Select **Security and Login** from the left-hand menu

3 Scroll down to the Two-Factor Authentication section, and select **Edit** next to **Use two-factor authentication**

4 Enter your password and click **Add phone number** next to Text Message (SMS) if you haven't already or, if you use an authentication app, opt to use this instead

5 You can also set up a backup method just in case something happens, such as you lose your phone. Next to **Recovery Codes** select **Setup**

6 Click **Get Codes**

7 Make a note of the codes and use them if you need to

8 You'll be asked if you want Facebook to remember your devices, ensuring codes are only needed in addition to passwords when you (or someone else) tries to log in to Facebook via an unrecognized device

You can change your password in the **Security and Login** section. Do this often, and make sure your passwords are hard to guess. Don't use your own name or familiar words; make passwords lengthy; and have a good mix of numbers, letters and symbols.

Take a privacy checkup (see page 171) and click **How to keep your account secure**. You'll be reminded of the need to choose a secure password, with the option to change yours. You can also choose to be notified if Facebook detects that your account is being accessed from a device it doesn't recognize. We strongly recommend you activate this.

Getting suspicious login alerts

If Facebook detects someone has logged in on a device or browser that you do not normally use, you can receive an alert.

Hot tip

If you do receive an alert and you do not recognize the device or browser, always change your password.

1 Click the downward arrow in the top-right corner of the screen, select **Settings & Privacy** then **Settings**

2 Select **Security and Login** from the left-hand menu

3 Scroll down to the **Setting up extra security** section and select **Edit** next to **Get alerts about unrecognized logins**

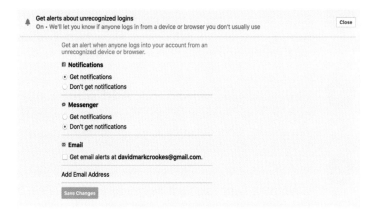

4 If you want the alert to be a Facebook notification, select the button next to **Get notifications**

5 You can also get alerts via Messenger

6 If you want the alert to be sent to your email address, click the button next to **Get email alerts at**

7 You can change the email address by clicking **Add Email Address**

8 Click **Save Changes**

Tackling a hacked account

Unfortunately, some people set up fake Facebook accounts in other people's names or manage to hack into an existing account. If this happens to you, there are some steps you can take.

Dealing with an imposter account

1 If you discover somebody is using your email address or phone number on an account that you have not set up, simply add that email address or phone number to your own account, and it will be removed from the other

2 If you discover somebody is pretending to be you, then visit the offending profile, click the three-dot **Menu** button on its cover photo, and select **Report**. Now, tell Facebook about your suspicions

Dealing with a hacked account

1 Should your account be compromised, go to **http://www.facebook.com/hacked**

2 Select why you think you have been hacked and click **Continue** so that Facebook can perform checks on your account and take you through the process of securing it

Ending an active hacking session

1 What if somebody is accessing your account right now? Click the downward arrow in the top-right corner, select **Settings & Privacy** and click **Settings**

2 Click **Security and login** in the left-hand menu

3 Look under the heading **Where you're logged in**. Click the three-dot **Menu** option to the right of the entries, and select **Not you?** or **Log out**

Only your friends will be able to see that you are safe, so don't worry about broadcasting your whereabouts to the wider public.

Marking yourself as safe

The world is not always as safe as it should be. Terrorism, natural disasters and terrifying incidents may touch our lives at any time. It can lead others to worry about your safety, regardless of whether you are in the midst of the crisis or simply in the vicinity. To help relieve stress and worry among your friends and family, Facebook has a Safety Check feature that allows you to indicate that you are okay. The function is activated by the Facebook community when an incident occurs. It will appear if a lot of people are discussing the incident in a particular area.

1 If you are in an affected area, Facebook will look at the area you have listed in your profile, determine if you are using the internet in that location and send you a message asking if you are safe

2 You are then given two options: **I'm safe** and **I'm not in the area**. You can select the most appropriate

3 If you mark yourself as safe, then this information will appear on your friends' News Feeds, and a notification will also be sent

4 Doing so can put other people's minds at ease, letting them know that you are okay. Likewise, you will be able to see if other people you know are safe too

Checking someone else is safe

1 Visit **facebook.com/crisisresponse**

2 Select a crisis

3 See if any friends are listed as being in the area or click **Search for a Friend**

4 You can also help by making a donation or creating a fundraiser. There are safety tips too

14 Using third-party apps

This brief chapter helps you make more of Facebook.

If you log in to a service using Facebook and later decide you don't want to do this, search online to see if the company will let you switch to a standard login. Some, such as Spotify, have help pages detailing such a process.

Hot tip

When signing up to an app or game, look for the **Edit This** button on the screen, which shows the information the app is set to receive. You can remove some of that information. See the opposite page for details of what can be changed. As you'll see, you can alter the app settings at any time.

Using Facebook as a login

Many websites and apps allow you to bypass the tedium of setting up a username and password in order to access them. Instead, they let you log in using your Facebook credentials, saving time and cutting the hassle of having to keep remembering your details.

Services that allow you to do this include the music-streaming site Spotify and the image-collecting network Pinterest. In fact, social logins have almost become the norm, so you are bound to encounter them at one point or another. Many love the modern convenience on offer.

Should I use it?

Facebook wants to be a trusted source for verifying your identity.

- It will never give a third party your Facebook password.

- It lets you benefit from its advanced security, which means it is more secure when logging in to small websites.

- It puts you in control, allowing you to delete your account with the third party with ease.

- But Facebook will typically provide the third party with your public profile (which means your name, profile picture, age range, gender, language and country) as well as your Friends list, email address and date of birth.

Signing up to a third-party service using Facebook

1 Taking Spotify as an example, go to **http://www.spotify.com** and click **Sign up**

2 Click **Sign Up With Facebook** and you can get around filling in your email address, password and date of birth by logging in to Facebook and letting your details be used

3 You'll now be able to select **Log In With Facebook** to access the service in future

Altering the app settings

You can fine-tune what you share with third-party apps. The only exception is that you are unable to prevent them from seeing your name, profile picture, cover photo, gender, networks, username and user ID.

Hot tip

As well as using the main method, you can click the downward arrow at the top of the Facebook screen, select **Security & Privacy** and choose **Privacy Checkup**. Choose **Your data settings on Facebook** and it will show you any apps and websites that use your Facebook account as a login. You can remove any you don't want to use.

Changing the permissions for third-party apps

1 Click the downward arrow in the top-right corner of the screen, select **Settings & Privacy** and click **Settings**

2 Click **Apps and Websites** from the left-hand menu

3 Any apps you have logged in to using Facebook appear at the top of the screen. You can tick the box next to any and click **Remove** or click **View and edit** to look at an app or website in greater detail

Kickstarter
Added on Aug 25, 2012   View and edit

4 You will see a list of information you are providing to the app. Move the slider to Off if there is anything you want to stop Facebook from sharing. Some info such as your name and profile image may be mandatory, which means you can't prevent it from being shared

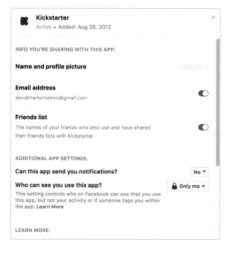

Kickstarter ×
Active • Added: Aug 25, 2012

INFO YOU'RE SHARING WITH THIS APP:

Name and profile picture   REQUIRED

Email address
davidmarkcrookes@gmail.com

Friends list
The names of your friends who also use and have shared their friends lists with Kickstarter

ADDITIONAL APP SETTINGS:

Can this app send you notifications?   No ▾
Who can see you use this app?   🔒 Only me ▾
This setting controls who on Facebook can see that you use this app, but not your activity or if someone tags you within the app. Learn More

LEARN MORE:

Hot tip

Keep scrolling down this panel and you'll see your User ID. Use this if you want to contact the app developer and ask how it is using your data.

5 Scroll down further, and choose whether or not you want the app to send you notifications through Facebook. Click **Save**

Controlling apps and games

You can change the settings in Facebook to prevent you from being able to log in to websites, applications or games using Facebook. You can also stop friends interacting with you using apps and websites.

1 Click the downward arrow in the top-right corner of the screen, select **Settings & Privacy** and click **Settings**

 **Apps, Websites and Games**

This setting controls your ability to interact with apps, websites and games both on and off Facebook.

2 Click **Apps and Websites** from the left-hand menu

Turned on

Edit

3 Select **Edit** in the box that is marked **Apps, Websites and Games**

4 Select **Turn Off**

Stopping game requests and app notifications
If you are fed up receiving invites to games such as Candy Crush Saga, you can call a halt to them.

1 Follow Steps 1 and 2 above

Game and App Notifications

This setting controls game requests from friends and game status updates, and app notifications from app developers on Facebook and Gameroom. Changing these settings will not impact your ability to use apps or play games.

Turned on

Edit

2 Click **Edit** in the box called **Game and App Notifications**

3 Select **Turn Off**

Index

R

S

T